THE BEST CARIBBEAN FOODS
TO COMBAT CHRONIC DISEASES

PRAISE FOR *THE BEST CARIBBEAN FOODS*
TO COMBAT CHRONIC DISEASES

Professor Fitzroy Henry and his team have effectively channelled their vast experience in public health nutrition to produce evidence-based dietary guidelines for making healthy food choices. This book is a significant tool in filling the knowledge gap that exists among consumers, scientists and policy makers who are often challenged by the need to differentiate between fad and facts around healthy eating and disease prevention.

The Best Caribbean Foods to Combat Chronic Diseases is replete with compelling historical details around the emergence of dietary patterns in the Caribbean, along with convenient tabulations of comparative nutrient rankings. This has rarely been seen for foods, particularly in the Caribbean. The attractive photographs combined with easy-to-understand nutritional composition and facts add to the food and nutrition literacy of the reader.

This book comes at a time when there is much confusion around healthy foods and presents a much-needed common sense approach to healthy eating. It is an essential requisite for understanding the science behind healthy food choices and hence gaining the upper hand in the battle against chronic diseases.

—*Professor **Dan Ramdath** formerly, Head – Department of Preclinical Sciences, University of the West Indies, St Augustine; Fellow of the American College of Nutrition; Adjunct Professor, University of Saskatchewan, Canada*

At long last, a factual, easy-to-understand summary of which real Caribbean foods can not only solve nutrition problems but reverse them! Ranking Caribbean foods by the food groups makes it easy for readers to prioritize the disease-reversing foods. Giving each food a 10-star rating based on nutritional criteria makes it easy for readers to understand how each food earned its rating. Showing a visual of each food makes it easy for all Caribbean readers to recognize the foods. No chance of mistaking Jamaican ackee for Barbadian ackee (Jamaican guinep)! If you are a health reader, head straight to the *Health and Dietary Benefits* section. If you want a quick summary, head straight to the *Nutritional Criteria and Rating* table for each food. This is just what the Caribbean needs! This should be required reading for all but especially in schools and colleges!

—***Dr Marcia Magnus**, Associate Professor of Dietetics and Nutrition, Florida International University, Miami, Florida, USA*

THE BEST
CARIBBEAN FOODS
TO COMBAT
CHRONIC DISEASES

FITZROY J. HENRY AND **JUNE HOLDIP**

University of Technology, Jamaica Press

First published in Jamaica 2021 by
University of Technology, Jamaica Press
237 Old Hope Road
Kingston 6
Email: utechjapress@utech.edu.jm

A catalogue record of this book is available from the
National Library of Jamaica.

ISBN: 978-976-96515-6-2 (print)
978-976-96515-7-9 (Kindle)

Cover and book design by Robert Harris
Email: roberth@cwjamaica.com

Set inMinion Pro 12/16 x 27

Printed in the USA.

CONTENTS

FOREWORD

Finally!

This book is what you never knew you were waiting for and is long overdue. In these days of globalisation and glorification of fast food, Caribbean people have been at risk of losing the appreciation of commonly used foods and their unique style of cooking.

This book, *The Best Caribbean Foods to Combat Chronic Diseases* is focused on ranking the healthiest foods to combat non-communicable diseases (NCDs), in particular, but to my delight, it is filled with unexpected snippets of what makes us Caribbean.

I learnt so much about the Caribbean culture, the history of the cooking practices of all of the ancestors from across the world who travelled, often against their will, to this corner of the world, this heaven on earth that we Caribbean people call home.

I found it difficult to put down, not only because of the writing style which is very Caribbean in its rhythm and relaxed tone, but more importantly because in its pages, I found some element of being Caribbean with which I could connect and smile as I recalled some experiences in my life as a Caribbean person and interactions with Caribbean people.

Now to focus on the real purpose. This is an excellent technical source for nutritionists and dietitians and other health practitioners, as well as a reference for foodies, or the person who needs to stick to a healthy diet for weight loss or control of a disease condition.

The surge in interest in cooking, because of the "lock down" to control the spread of the illnesses during the COVID-19 pandemic, makes for opportune timing of the release of this book. And as NCDs and obesity have proven to be risk factors for contracting the more severe forms of COVID-19 disease, people need to read this book to understand the healing properties of good fresh food in all times, with COVID-19 and even after a vaccine becomes accessible.

Readers certainly will begin to appreciate the way fresh food is inextricably linked to the flavour of Caribbean dishes and why Caribbean people have woven cooking into celebrations of all aspects of our lives, especially rites of passage; from the introduction of solid food to the infant to the post burial repast.

One of the fun surprises about this book is that it tells the story of the creativity and surprising innovation of our ancestors and how this has passed down to us 21st century Caribbean people. Our ancestors let no part of the food crop and some animal products go to waste. From clothing to medicine, there was no wastage of leaves or roots or flowers of our food crops, neither was there any aspect of the human condition which was not improved or cured or made easier to endure through the varied use of food plants. Most of that is described right here in this book. As the Caribbean has developed a high prevalence of obesity even in our children and NCDs throughout our populations, we need this book to get us back to the first principles of selecting, preparing and enjoying tasty food which promotes NCD-free life.

The Caribbean is a melting pot of peoples and cultures which have boiled down to what makes us unique and recognisable wherever we go.

Much like how proper pepper pot is made and kept safe to eat by using cassareep, there has to be a common denominator which holds the myriad aspects of being Caribbean together, which gives meaning to the Caribbean way of life and makes everything better.

Perhaps this book is defining that essence of being Caribbean – our fresh food and the unique way we prepare it in order to preserve the health of the Caribbean people.

Happy reading. Happy and healthy eating.

DR JOY ST JOHN
Executive Director
Caribbean Public Health Agency (CARPHA)

PREFACE

The aim of this book is to provide a wealth of easily understood information that will help consumers make healthy choices when purchasing, preparing and consuming foods. Although food is generally for satisfying appetite and for pleasure, it should also be for improving nutrition and health. The tsunami of obesity and NCDs is largely diet-related hence it behoves individuals, families and the general public to know the nutritional content and value of commonly consumed foods. This book is a boon to the dietary guidelines currently being implemented in many Caribbean countries because it provides a ranking of foods from within the Six Caribbean Food Groups which form the basis of all national guidelines. The cost of individual items can now be balanced with the nutrient content of the food items.

It is true that how foods are combined and prepared will determine whether a diet becomes less or more nutritious. Therefore, choosing a healthy starting point is essential– hence the need to know the nutrient value of the foods. This is not a recipe book. Several excellent Caribbean cookbooks are currently available. The focus here is not on *how* we cook but on *what* we cook.

The book uses the latest scientific information on macronutrients, micronutrients, phytochemicals and zoochemicals as they relate to the most important public health challenge in the region – non-communicable diseases such as diabetes, hypertension, heart disease and cancer, among others. In the book each food item is presented with an attractive image, nutrient content and engaging and remarkable facts and features. It is a concise visual and factual celebration of the best Caribbean foods linked to their unique health and dietary benefits. With profiles of the highest ranked fruits, vegetables, foods from animals, legumes, nuts and seeds, fats and oils and staples, this compilation also provides insights into each food's distinctive history in relation to Caribbean cuisine and culture.

The book highlights Caribbean foods that have been traditionally used for many ailments. However, persons with medical conditions should use this information strictly under the guidance of qualified medical professionals.

Students at all levels can read, think and explore the history and cultural origins of commonly consumed foods. Teachers of courses on food security, nutrition, agriculture, social studies and health sciences will find this a source for creative class activities and opportunities for cross-curricular learning experiences. There is vital information about preparation and common culinary uses and food products manufactured by the food industry. Most importantly, the book presents critical information on everyday foods to help the general public choose more healthfully. Food holds a vital place in our lives as it is far more than providing sustenance. It defines us. It has the power to heal our bodies and minds. What we eat therefore deserves extraordinary attention.

In short, the book uses a system that mirrors simplified food labels that can help consumers be mindful about their food choices and ultimately their eating habits. Hopefully it will help the reader to go beyond the lovely taste and texture of Caribbean foods and expose the marvellous content of their ingredients.

PROFESSOR FITZROY J. HENRY
College of Health Sciences,
University of Technology, Jamaica

ACKNOWLEDGEMENTS

The authors are indebted to the numerous researchers and scientists around the world who conducted the original studies and systematic reviews to provide the rich information used in this book. The bibliographies at the end of each section credit the major sources used. Any omissions are regretted.

Sections of this book received invaluable contributions from the following persons:

- Beverly Lawrence (Methods) has over 30 years of experience covering the areas of agricultural and economic planning, food and nutrition security and public health with a strong focus on policy analysis, program development and evaluation. Her career has been centred on research, policy and program analysis in food security, and nutrition in the region.
- Deonne Caines (Foods from Animals and Fats and Oils) has worked in the field of Nutrition since 2011. While working at the Caribbean Food and Nutrition Institute (CFNI) she was involved with research and various aspects of policy development and program planning, implementation and monitoring at the national level in several Caribbean countries. She obtained her BSc in Basic Medical Sciences and an MSc in Nutrition, both from the University of the West Indies, Mona.
- Sheerin Eyre (Fruits and Vegetables) originally from Lahore, Pakistan, now resides in Jamaica. She is an author, registered Nutritionist and employed as a Senior Lecturer in the College of Health Sciences at the University of Technology, Jamaica. She coordinates the Wellness Centre, which offers lifestyle enhancing programs in nutrition, fitness and wellness to the University community.
- Melissa Nelson used her photographic skills to produce some of the illustrations.

INTRODUCTION

Heart disease, cancer, diabetes and other non-communicable diseases (NCDs) are currently the biggest threat to Caribbean health. They also threaten the economic security of individuals and countries in the Region. Diet is a major part of the development of the NCD problem. Diet is also a major part of the solution. This book highlights some of the best Caribbean foods that can help to combat NCDs based on recent empirical evidence.

THE EVIDENCE

The World Health Organization (WHO) defines a healthy diet as one which optimizes health and provides nutrients in adequate quantities to support and sustain life and prevent illnesses (WHO, 2018). To achieve this goal, researchers have recently proposed reference diets which outline the types and amount of food and nutrients necessary to guide policy makers, businesses, food manufacturers and the general population (Willett et al., 2019).

If used as proposed, these diets can substantially reduce the risk of developing non-communicable diseases in the Caribbean. But what foods should be selected and what are their nutritional profiles? This book answers this question by providing information on commonly consumed Caribbean foods.

In ranking the foods, the book utilized relevant recent empirical evidence as indicated in the findings below:

LIST OF RECENT FINDINGS

- Animal sources of protein are usually found in foods in conjunction with fat and other constituents which may affect health negatively (Willett et al., 2019).

- All evidence points to plant-based diets with the inclusion of little red meats (USDA, 2015).
- Red meats have been associated with total mortality and increased risk of stroke (Chen et al., 2012) and type II diabetes (Feskens et al., 2013).
- Processed red meats have been associated with increased risk of death from any cause and cardiovascular disease (Abete et al., 2014).
- Processed red meats have also been listed as a group one carcinogen by the International Agency for Research on Cancer (IARC); while unprocessed red meats fall in group two (IARC, 2019).
- Replacing protein from animal sources with protein from plant sources has been associated with reduced overall mortality (Song et al., 2016).
- Vegetarian diets have been associated with lower overall mortality risk than omnivore diets (Orlich et al., 2013).
- Much of the benefits from legumes and nuts include improved blood lipid concentrations, reduced oxidative stress, inflammation, visceral adiposity, hyperglycemia and insulin resistance (Kris-Etherton et al., 2008; Sabaté, 2010).
- Nuts are helpful in weight management as they induce satiety and are associated with relatively no weight gain, reduced weight, and reduced risk of obesity (Grosso & Estruch, 2016).
- Legumes have been associated with reduced LDL cholesterol levels and blood pressure (Kushi et al., 1999).
- Legumes lower the risk of coronary heart disease (Afshin et al., 2014).
- Refined grains are noted for their high glycemic index, increased risk of adverse health effect and weight gain (Willett et al., 2019; Mozaffarian et al., 2011).
- Higher intakes of fruits and vegetables have been recommended by WHO (2018) as a natural source of sugars and also because they contain many vitamins, minerals, bioactive compounds and dietary fibre.
- Fruits and vegetables are associated with improved cardiovascular outcomes (Wang et al., 2014), reduced blood pressure (Binia et al., 2015), and reduced risk of type II diabetes (Muraki et al., 2015).
- Saturated fats should be replaced with unsaturated vegetable oils that are high in polyunsaturated fats inclusive of omega-3 and omega-6 (Wang et al., 2016).

- Trans fat consumption is injurious to health and wellness and should be avoided (Mozaffarian et al., 2006).

This book utilizes recent research findings and refers to the various food items which may be included in the diet to improve consumers' health. Further, by ranking the food items within each food group, it is hoped that policy makers responsible for food production will include the health dimension as a priority when developing national food strategies.

THE RANKING OF FOODS

The criteria for ranking the foods and associations with non-communicable diseases (NCDs) are stated in Table 1. These are general recommendations for the level of intake based on proven or probable associations between nutrients and diseases.

Table 1: Criteria for Ranking Foods and the Associations with Major NCDs

Criteria for Ranking	Associations with Major NCDs
High in Complex Carbohydrates	• Greater glycaemic control due to lower glycaemic index, reducing risk of impaired glucose tolerance, the precursor to onset of diabetes mellitus; • More satiety and fewer calories, allowing for better weight management
High in Dietary Fibre	• Reduces plasma total and LDL cholesterol levels, reducing risk of cardiovascular diseases (CVDs); • Reduces transit time through the gut, possibly lowering absorption of carcinogens.
Low in Cholesterol	• Reduces the risk of plaque build-up within blood vessel walls and thus contributes to cardiovascular diseases; • Reduces impaired glucose tolerance and dyslipidaemia.
Low in Saturated Fats	• Reduces risk of elevated total and LDL cholesterol levels; • Reduces risk of fat-induced impaired glucose tolerance and insulin sensitivity; • Reduces risk of obesity and its co-morbidities.
High in Monounsaturated Fats	• Reduces risk of elevated total and LDL cholesterol; • Reduces risk of impaired glucose tolerance.

Criteria for Ranking	Associations with Major NCDs
High in Polyunsaturated Fats	• Reduces the risk of coronary heart disease.
High in Iron	• Reduces risk of iron-deficiency anaemia; • Reduces the risk of impaired cognitive function.
Low in Sodium	• Reduces risk of elevated blood pressure and coronary heart disease (CHD.)
High in Potassium	• Reduces risk of elevated blood pressure and CHD.
High in Calcium	• Reduces risk of osteopenia and osteoporosis.
High in Vitamin A	• Promotes the body's use of iron; • Reduces the risk of blindness and ocular injury; • Reduces the risk of impaired growth and development and of impaired immunocompetence.
High in Vitamin C	• Facilitates iron-absorption; • Possibly lowers the risk of cancer and CVDs.
High in Vitamin B_6	• Assists the release of glycogen for energy from the liver; • Enables the body to manufacture and convert amino acids and metabolize proteins.
High in Folate	• Promotes DNA synthesis and cell replication to probably decrease the risk of certain cancers and CVDs; • Aids in reducing blood homocysteine levels.
Phytochemicals	• May lower the risk of certain cancers, diabetes, high blood pressure, and heart disease.
Zoochemicals	• Modifies multiple physiological functions including anti-inflammatory, antihypertension and antimicrobial actions

Source: Food and Nutrition Security Factors and Criteria for Prioritization: Nutrition and Health Perspective (PAHO/CFNI, 2010)

To determine what percentage of the Recommended Dietary Allowances (*%RDA*) contributed by each food, the quantity of the nutrient contained in the food was divided by the RDA for that nutrient. This process was repeated for each nutrient considered.

Annex 1 shows how the RDA values were selected for the different sexes and age groups. Where RDAs have not been established, the WHO Recommended Population Nutrient Intake Goals (PGs), shown in Annex 2, were used to determine the percentage of the PG (*%PG*) contributed by 100 grams of each food.

The criteria for scoring the nutrient contribution and other dietary components using the %RDA and %PG values are shown in Table 2 (page 6). The nutrients were scored in one of two groups, namely Block A or Block B. Block A scores the nutrients that are favourable to health goals and Block B scores the nutrients that are less favourable to health goals. In Block A, the higher the percentage contribution to the RDA, the higher the score allocated with 10 being the highest. In contrast, with Block B, the higher the percentage contribution to the RDA, the lower the score assigned, with zero (0) being the lowest.

Using the %RDA and % PG values, a third ranking based on weighted values was added to highlight nutrients that significantly influence (increase or decrease) nutritional health. Criteria for ranking of weighted values were based on the strength of scientific evidence as presented in the *2003 WHO/ FAO. Diet, Nutrition and the Prevention of Chronic Diseases Technical Report Series, No. 916 and Food, Nutrition, Physical Activity and the Prevention of Cancer: A Global Perspective (2007)*; Willett et al (2019).

Nutrients that have been shown to decrease the risk of observed health conditions were awarded a positive figure: (1) being possible; (2) being probable and (3) being convincing. Conversely, nutrients that increase risk received a negative point (1–3) depending on the strength of evidence. Nutrients contained in each category were only eligible for this grading criterion if it had a %RDA or % PG value of 20 or greater. This criterion was based on the U.S. Food and Drug Administration Food Labelling Guidelines (2004).

Application of the above criteria along with the Six Caribbean Food Groups were used as the reference to rank foods thus providing a more balanced picture in terms of the items selected from each Food Group.

SCORING FOODS BASED ON THE POTENTIAL FOR ADDED HEALTH BENEFITS

While most foods are good to maintain a healthy diet, not all contain powerful components such as *phytochemicals* that can further fight disease and improve the immune system. These are often called "superfoods". The term superfood is misused as a marketing pitch. In this book we highlight their additional active compounds but do not undermine the traditional nutritional quality of the foods. Due to the noted characteristics of superfoods

Table 2: Scoring Nutrient Contributions of Foods Based on % RDA and % PG

BLOCK A: [i]Foods Favoured in High Amounts			BLOCK B: [ii]Foods Favoured in Low Amounts		
Score	If Nutrient Contribution is:	Comment:	Score	If Nutrient Contribution is:	Comment:
10	> 50%	If the standard amount is consumed twice daily, the nutrient goal will be met.	10	< 5%	Negligible; Contains no appreciable amount. The standard amount may be consumed up to 20 times daily before the nutrient goal is exceeded.
8	33.1–50.0%	If the standard amount is consumed 2–3 times daily, the nutrient goal will be met.	8	5.1–10.0%	The standard amount may be consumed up to 10 times daily before the nutrient goal is exceeded.
6	20.1–33.0%	If the standard amount is consumed 4–5 times daily, the nutrient goal will be met.	6	10.1–33.0%	The standard amount may be consumed 3–10 times daily before the nutrient goal is exceeded.
4	10.1–20.0%	If the standard amount is consumed 5–10 times daily, the nutrient goal will be met.	4	33.1–50.0%	The standard amount may be consumed 2–3 times daily before the nutrient goal is exceeded.
2	5.1–10.0%	If the standard amount is consumed 10–20 times daily, the nutrient goal will be met.	2	50.1–75.0%	The standard amount may be consumed 1–2 times daily before the nutrient goal is exceeded.
0	< 5%	Negligible; Contains no appreciable amount. If the standard amount is consumed at least 20 times daily the nutrient goal will be met.	0	> 75%	The standard amount may be consumed once daily before the nutrient goal is exceeded.
Score 10 used to denote >50% contribution			Score 0 used to denote >75% contribution		

Score 10 used to denote >50% contribution
[i]Dietary Fibre; Complex Carbohydrates; Monounsaturated Fats; Polyunsaturated Fats Iron; Potassium; Calcium; Vitamin A; Vitamin C; Vitamin B_6; Folate

Score 0 used to denote >75% contribution
[ii]Total Fat; Cholesterol; Saturated Fats; Sodium

Source: Food and Nutrition Security Factors and Criteria for Prioritization: Nutrition and Health Perspective (PAHO/CFNI, 2010)

there has been an explosion of consumer interest in the health enhancing role of specific foods or physiologically-active food components, now known as functional foods (Crowe, 2013).

Many plant-based diets have components other than the traditional nutrients that can reduce the risk of several chronic diseases (Slavin 2012). More than a dozen classes of these biologically active plant chemicals, known as *phytochemicals*, have been identified. (Steinmetz, 1991) For example, regarding cancers, overwhelming evidence from hundreds of studies indicate that cancer risk in people consuming diets high in fruits and vegetables was only one-half compared with those consuming few of these foods. (Block, 1992). Health professionals have increasingly recognized the role of phytochemicals in health enhancement (Gordon, 2012). Beyond cancer, some key phytochemicals have several other benefits, for example:

- *isoflavones* are known to have anti-diabetes properties;
  antioxidants may have anticancer effects;
- *flavanols* in general promote heart health and may help reduce stroke risk, and flavanols such as quercetin decrease oxidative stress and have anti-cancer activity.
- *Catecholamines* help with anti-inflammatory activity. (Arts, 2005; Erdman 2007).

Some animal foods have zoochemicals which are reported to assist body functions. In recognition of the importance of these phytochemicals and zoochemicals, they have been added to the traditional nutritional criteria for each related food. Annex 3 shows that apart from Vegetables and Fruits, other plant-based foods have the potential to confer additional health benefits. In the book the foods are presented in each food group by rank. The rank was determined not only by the total score for each food but also by a weight given for each criterion based on the "list of recent findings" presented above.

WHAT DOES THIS MEAN FOR FOOD SELECTION?

The foods included in this book are only a small selection of foods available across the Caribbean. Only ten foods have been included for each food group, representing the top ten according to evidence available at the time of compilation. This should not be interpreted to mean that foods that were not included are unhealthy or that healthy diets should only include the foods in this book.

A healthy diet is one which includes a wide variety of foods and provides all the nutrients in appropriate quantities. In addition, focusing on unprocessed and minimally processed foods and keeping intake of processed and ultraprocessed foods to a minimum will help to control intake of trans fats, saturated fat, sodium and added sugars. Food preparation methods should also aim to do the same.

The aim is to help consumers to choose especially in circumstances where choices are limited by finances or availability or where the consumer has special dietary needs. When treating or managing medical conditions, the information in this book should be used under the guidance of qualified professionals, e.g. medical doctors, nutritionists and dietitians.

ANNEX 1

RECOMMENDED DIETARY ALLOWANCES[1] USED TO DETERMINE THE PERCENTAGE CONTRIBUTION OF SELECTED NUTRIENTS

Selected Nutrients	Recommended Dietary Allowances				
	Ages 19–29 years		Ages 30–60 years		[i]RDA Values Used in Analysis (Ages 19–60 years)
	Males	Females	Males	Females	Males & Females
Iron (mg)	10	15	10	15	**15**
Sodium (mg)	500	500	500	500	**500**
Potassium (mg)	2000	2000	2000	2000	**2000**
Calcium (mg)	700	700	700	700	**700**
Vitamin A (μg RAE)	650	560	650	560	**650**
Vitamin C (mg)	60	60	60	60	**60**
Vitamin B$_6$ (mg)	0.7	0.8	0.7	0.8	**0.8**
Folate (mg)	200	200	200	200	**200**

[i]Higher of the two RDA values used; no risk of toxicity at these intake levels

1   **RDA values** derived from: *Caribbean Food and Nutrition Institute (1994). Recommended Dietary Allowances for the Caribbean, 1993 Revision. CFNI*, 1994 Kingston, Jamaica.

ANNEX 2

POPULATION NUTRIENT INTAKE GOALS[2] USED TO DETERMINE THE PERCENTAGE CONTRIBUTION OF SELECTED NUTRIENTS

Dietary Factor	PG (% of total energy)
Total Fat[ii]	15–30%
Saturated fatty acids	<10%
Trans fatty acids	<1%
Cholesterol	<300 mg per day
Monounsaturated fatty acids (MUFAs)	By difference[iii]
Polyunsaturated fatty acids (PUFAs)	6–10%
Total Carbohydrate[iv]	55–75%
Dietary Fibre	>25 g per day

[i]Assumed total daily energy intake at 2250 kcal – sufficient to meet basic nutrition need
[ii]1 gram of fat contributes approximately 9 kcal of energy
[iii]Total fat – (saturated fat + trans fat + polyunsaturated fat)
[iv]PG for total carbohydrate used as PG for complex carbohydrates – preferable form of carbohydrate to meet energy and nutrient needs

---

2   **Population goals** derived from: WHO (2003). WHO/ FAO. Diet, Nutrition and the Prevention of Chronic Diseases Technical report Series, No. 916. Geneva; CFNI (2010). Population Nutrient Intake Goals for the Caribbean (2010).

ANNEX 3

SELECTED CARIBBEAN FOODS WITH NON-TRADITIONAL
POTENTIAL HEALTH BENEFITS

Foods	Scientific Name	Some Phytochemical Constituents	Overall Therapeutic Indications
Ackee	*Blighia sapida*	Alkaloids, tannins, saponins, flavonoids and phenols	Antioxidant activity
Avocado	*Persea americana*	Isoflavones, Lutein, zeaxanthin, saponin, genestein	Helps support cardiovascular health; anticancer activity; boosts immune system
Banana – Green/Ripe	*Musa acuminate, Musa sapientum*	Catecholamines, tannin, albuminoids, glycosides, alkaloids, flavonoids; quercetin, sterols	Antidiarrhoeal; Ulcer protective antimicrobial activity; wound healing, kidney anti-cancer activities
Breadfruit	*Artocarpus altilis*	Flavonoids including geranyl	Cytoprotection; Anti-cancer; antioxidant activities
Cassava	*Manihot esculenta*	Alkaloids, saponins, steroids, flavonoids; Flavonols	Cytoprotection; wound healing
Coconut	*Cocos nucifera*	Terpenoids, alkaloids, lauric acid, glycosides and steroids; flavanoids, phenols, steroids	Glucose homeostasis and antioxidant activity; controls severe hyperglycaemia
Corn	*Zea mays*	Phenols; Lutein, Zeaxanthin;free Stanols/Sterols; anthocyanins	Controls diabetes, lowers blood pressure; anticancer activities
Dasheen	*Colocasia esculenta*	Thiamin, folate, calcium oxalate	Management of diabetic nephropathy.

ANNEX 3: SELECTED CARIBBEAN FOODS WITH NON-TRADITIONAL POTENTIAL HEALTH BENEFITS *(Cont'd)*

Foods	Scientific Name	Some Phytochemical Constituents	Overall Therapeutic Indications
Kidney Beans (Red)	*Phaseolus vulgaris*	flavonoids, unsaturated sterols, saponins,	Hypoglycaemic, antidiabetic properties, appetite control
Oats – rolled	*Avena sativa*	Phenolic compounds, flavonoids, sterols	Lowers LDL cholesterol and blood pressure; improved insulin sensitivity
Peas – Pigeon (Gungo Peas)	*Cajanus cajan*	Sitosterol, isoquercitrin, quercetin	Anti-inflammatory, antioxidant, Immuno-modulatory activities
Peas – Split	*Pisum sativum*	phenolic acids, flavone and flavonol glycoside	Antioxidant activity
Plantain – Green /Ripe	*Musa paradisiaca*	Serotonin, Flavonoids, Acyl steryl glycosides	Gastroprotective; lowers cholesterol; antioxidant; mutagenic effect
Potato, Irish	*Solanum tuberosum*	Phenols, carotenoids, anthocyanins	Reduces blood pressure and cancer cell growth
Potato, sweet –purple	*Ipomoea batatas*	Anthocyanin, Quercetin, steroids, Flavonoids, Polyphenols	Antioxidant; anticancer activities
Rice, brown	*Oryza sativa*	Phenols, Phytic acid	Cancer prevention
Yam	*Dioscorea spp*	Phenols	Lowers LDL cholesterol and colon cancer risk

BIBLIOGRAPHY

Abete, I., Romaguera, D., Vieira, A., Lopez de Munain, A., & Norat, T. (2014). Association between total, processed, red and white meat consumption and all-cause, CVD and IHD mortality: a meta-analysis of cohort studies. *British Journal of Nutrition, 112*(5), 762–775. doi: 10.1017/s000711451400124x

Afshin, A., Micha, R., Khatibzadeh, S., & Mozaffarian, D. (2014). Consumption of nuts and legumes and risk of incident ischemic heart disease, stroke, and diabetes: a systematic review and meta-analysis. *The American Journal of Clinical Nutrition, 100*(1), 278–288. doi: 10.3945/ajcn.113.076901

Arts IC, Hollman PC (2005) Polyphenols and disease risk in epidemiologic studies. *Am J Clin Nutr* 81: 317S-325S.

Binia, A., Jaeger, J., Hu, Y., Singh, A., & Zimmermann, D. (2015). Daily potassium intake and sodium-to-potassium ratio in the reduction of blood pressure. *Journal of Hypertension, 33*(8), 1509–1520. doi: 10.1097/hjh.0000000000000611

Block G, Patterson B, Subar A (1992) Fruit, vegetables, and cancer prevention: a review of the epidemiological evidence. *Nutr Cancer* 18: 1–29.

Chen, G., Lv, D., Pang, Z., & Liu, Q. (2012). Red and processed meat consumption and risk of stroke: a meta-analysis of prospective cohort studies. *European Journal of Clinical Nutrition, 67*(1), 91–95. doi: 10.1038/ejcn.2012.180

Crowe KM, Francis C; Academy of Nutrition and Dietetics (2013) Position of the academy of nutrition and dietetics: functional foods. *J Acad Nutr Diet* 113: 1096-1103

Erdman JW Jr, Balentine D, Arab L, Beecher G, Dwyer JT, et al. (2007) Flavonoids and heart health: proceedings of the ILSI North America Flavonoids Workshop, May 31–June 1, 2005, Washington, DC. *J Nutr* 137: 718S-737S

Feskens, E., Sluik, D., & van Woudenbergh, G. (2013). Meat Consumption, Diabetes, and Its Complications. *Current Diabetes Reports, 13*(2), 298–306. doi: 10.1007/s11892-013-0365-0

Gordon MH (2012) Significance of dietary antioxidants for health. *Int J Mol Sci* 13:173-179.

Grosso, G., & Estruch, R. (2016). Nut consumption and age-related disease. *Maturitas, 84*, 11–16. doi: 10.1016/j.maturitas.2015.10.014

International Agency for Research on Cancer. (2019). *IARC Monographs on the Identification of Carcinogenic Hazards to Humans.* International Agency for Research on Cancer (WHO). Retrieved from https://monographs.iarc.fr/agents-classified-by-the-iarc/

Kris-Etherton, P., Hu, F., Ros, E., & Sabaté, J. (2008). The Role of Tree Nuts and Peanuts in the Prevention of Coronary Heart Disease: Multiple Potential Mechanisms. *The Journal of Nutrition, 138*(9), 1746S-1751S. doi: 10.1093/jn/138.9.1746s

Kushi, L., Meyer, K., & Jacobs, D. (1999). Cereals, legumes, and chronic disease risk reduction: evidence from epidemiologic studies. *The American Journal of Clinical Nutrition, 70*(3), 451s-458s. doi: 10.1093/ajcn/70.3.451s

Mozaffarian, D., Katan, M., Ascherio, A., Stampfer, M., & Willett, W. (2006). Trans Fatty Acids and Cardiovascular Disease. *Obstetrical & Gynecological Survey*, 61(8), 525–526. doi: 10.1097/01.ogx.0000228706.09374.e7

Mozaffarian, D., Hao, T., Rimm, E., Willett, W., & Hu, F. (2011). Changes in Diet and Lifestyle and Long-Term Weight Gain in Women and Men. *New England Journal of Medicine*, 364(25), 2392–2404. doi: 10.1056/nejmoa1014296

Muraki, I., Imamura, F., Manson, J., Hu, F., Willett, W., van Dam, R., & Sun, Q. (2013). Fruit consumption and risk of type 2 diabetes: results from three prospective longitudinal cohort studies. *BMJ*, 347(aug28 1), f5001–f5001. doi: 10.1136/bmj.f5001

Orlich, M., Singh, P., Sabaté, J., Jaceldo-Siegl, K., Fan, J., & Knutsen, S. et al. (2013). Vegetarian Dietary Patterns and Mortality in Adventist Health Study 2. *JAMA Internal Medicine*, 173(13), 1230. doi: 10.1001/jamainternmed.2013.6473

PAHO/CFNI (2010). Caribbean Food and Nutrition Institute The Contribution of CFNI to Caribbean Development 2001–2010. (CFNI, 2011).

Sabaté, J. (2010). Nut Consumption and Blood Lipid Levels. *Archives of Internal Medicine*, 170(9), 821. doi: 10.1001/archinternmed.2010.79

Slavin JL, Lloyd B (2012) Health benefits of fruits and vegetables. *AdvNutr* 3: 506–516.

Song, M., Fung, T., Hu, F., Willett, W., Longo, V., Chan, A., & Giovannucci, E. (2016). Association of Animal and Plant Protein Intake With All-Cause and Cause-Specific Mortality. *JAMA Internal Medicine*, 176(10), 1453. doi: 10.1001/jamainternmed.2016.4182

Steinmetz KA, Potter JD (1991) Vegetables, fruit, and cancer. II. Mechanisms. *Cancer Causes Control* 2: 427–442.

US Department of Agriculture, US Department of Health and Human Services. Scientific report of the 2015 Dietary Guidelines Advisory Committee. Washington, DC: US Government Printing Offices, 2015.

Wang, X., Ouyang, Y., Liu, J., Zhu, M., Zhao, G., Bao, W., & Hu, F. (2014). Fruit and vegetable consumption and mortality from all causes, cardiovascular disease, and cancer: systematic review and dose-response meta-analysis of prospective cohort studies. *BMJ*, 349(jul29 3), g4490–g4490. doi: 10.1136/bmj.g4490

Wang, D., Li, Y., Chiuve, S., Stampfer, M., Manson, J., & Rimm, E. et al. (2016). Association of Specific Dietary Fats With Total and Cause-Specific Mortality. *JAMA Internal Medicine*, 176(8), 1134. doi: 10.1001/jamainternmed.2016.2417

Willett, W., Rockström, J., Loken, B., Springmann, M., Lang, T., & Vermeulen, S. et al. (2019). Food in the Anthropocene: the EAT–Lancet Commission on healthy diets from sustainable food systems. *The Lancet*, 393(10170), 447–492. doi: 10.1016/s0140-6736(18)31788-4

World Health Organization. (2018). *A Healthy Diet*. World Health Organization. Retrieved from https://www.who.int/news-room/fact-sheets/detail/healthy-diet.

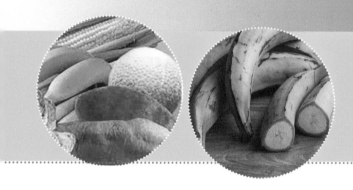

Staples are the dominant portion of the Caribbean diet, but they do require other foods to provide the additional energy, protein and nutrients that the body needs. In Caribbean countries the Staples Food Group is comprised of starchy fruits, roots, tubers, their by-products, and cereals. The non-cereal subgroup comprises green bananas, plantain, breadfruit, yam, potato, dasheen, coco, cassava, among others. The cereal subgroup consists of bread, flour and flour products, cornmeal, cooked and ready-to-eat cereals, macaroni, spaghetti, and rice, among others. The main nutrients contributed by both subgroups are carbohydrates, vitamins, minerals and fibre. Cereal grains are notably rich sources of B vitamins, vitamin E, and many minerals, such as iron, zinc, magnesium, and phosphorus.

Yam is a common *starchy staple* in the Caribbean and is one of the oldest, nutritious, versatile, and delicious foods. Yams are part of a rich social and religious heritage in West Africa. The African word Nyam which means "food" was devised from yam, a major food in some parts of the continent. In many areas of West Africa, yam remains the only crop that requires special ceremonies for its planting and harvest. Births, weddings, deaths and the installation of leaders and other people in high places are occasions that call for yam dishes. Little wonder that the slaves brought this prized food with them to the West Indies. Today, the chief yam producing regions are

West Africa, South-east Asia and the Caribbean together with parts of tropical America.

The other typical *cereal staple* in the Caribbean is rice. Whatever the country, rice is used almost every day as a standard dish with the main meal whether at mid-day or in the evening. Rice is cultivated in many English-speaking Caribbean countries as well as Puerto Rico, Cuba, and the Dominican Republic – islands and countries with warm temperatures and abundant annual rainfall. Vast rice paddies resemble grass-filled swamps in valleys, flatlands or lowlands. Yields are used for both local consumption and export. Rice comes in many varieties, it is versatile, nutritious, has many other health benefits, can also be included in many diets and is used by persons of various age groups.

RANK #1 – GREEN PLANTAIN

Nutritional Criteria	Rating
High in Complex Carbohydrates	★★★★★★★★★
High in Dietary Fibre	★★★★★★★
Low in Saturated Fats	★★★★★★★★★
High in Monounsaturated Fats	0
High in Polyunsaturated Fats	0
High in Iron	0
Low in Sodium	★★★★★★★★★
High in Potassium	★★★★★★★
High in Calcium	0
High in Vitamin A	★★★★★★
High in Vitamin C	★★★★★★
High in Vitamin B6	★★★★★★★
High in Folate	★★
Phytochemicals	★★★★

GREEN PLANTAIN

Scientific Name: *Plantago lanceolate*
Other Common Names: Spanish psyllium, French psyllium, blond plantago, Indian plantago

Origin and Background

The plant is believed to have originated in Southeast Asia. Plantains are native to India and the Caribbean. Plantains resemble bananas but they are longer and thicker skinned. They are often used as a substitute for other starchy foods. They are available either green, ripe or very ripe when the skin is usually black.

Varieties

There are about 250 species of plantains. When **green,** the edible portion is very firm, starchy, and not very sweet. **Yellow plantains** are mature and sweet. **Black** or **very ripe plantains** are the sweetest and softest. Plantains are sometimes referred to as a "starchy vegetable" but in the Caribbean, this food item is included in the Staples (Starchy) Food Group, one of the Six Caribbean Food Groups.

Health and Dietary Benefits

Green plantains are a rich source of fibre, vitamins A, C, and B$_6$, and the minerals magnesium and potassium. Plantains are a very good source of complex carbohydrates. They provide several health benefits and don't contain any significant levels of toxins. Some people have plantain allergies that cause itching and swelling of the lips, tongue and throat shortly after consumption.

Plantains are great for the immune system because they contain vitamin A which helps to control the immune response to battle illness. Vitamin A is also important for healthy skin, cell growth and the healing of wounds. Plantains are high in dietary fibre which is excellent for the digestive system. Dietary fibre helps with relieving constipation and provides some relief for haemorrhoids. Fibre also aids with weight control and is also beneficial for lowering blood cholesterol and blood pressure.

Plantains are rich in potassium, a mineral that is important for the functioning of many organs. Potassium helps to balance the effects of sodium, and hence beneficial for optimal heart health. Potassium is also important for the health of skeletal and smooth muscle contraction. High potassium levels may protect people from stroke, renal (kidney) disease and osteoporosis (weak and brittle bones). In addition, plantains are also a fair source of magnesium which has an important function in biochemical reactions in the body.

Preparation and Culinary Uses

Plantains are very versatile but must be cooked before they are eaten. Plantains can be baked, boiled, grilled, roasted, fried, mashed or chopped. They can also be used as an ingredient in stews and soups, steam-cooked for the elderly, dried and ground into flour to which milk can be added and used as cooked cereal (porridge) for infants and adults. When deep-fried, green plantains are enjoyed as chips, a popular snack all over the world. Deep-fried ripe or black plantain is also a popular side-dish. Other ingredients can be added to mashed ripe plantain to make fritters, pancakes or other creative dishes.

Other Uses

Parts of the plantain tree are also used for practical purposes. Flour made from plantain peel is a particularly good source of antioxidants, dietary fibre and can be used to make cookies. Plantain flowers are commonly used as food in countries like Vietnam, Laos and the Philippines. The flowers are used on salads or raw in vermicelli soup. In South India, there is also a type of dry curry called *poriyal* made from plantain flowers. In Central and South America, plantain leaves wrap tamales before and during cooking, as well as seasoned meats to preserve the flavor. In Africa, plantain leaves are used to wrap various ingredients to keep them intact while preparing things like corn dough and bean cakes. As an important part of many Hindu religious rituals, plantain leaves are used as plates and add a subtle hint of flavor to the dishes.

Plantain shoots are also harvested after the crop is picked. The layers of the plant can be removed like an onion, chopped and added to salads. The shoots can also be used to make wet or dry curries. The fibres from the shoots are also used as a weaving material to make rugs, mats and wrapping papers.

RANK #2 – YAM

Nutritional Criteria	Rating
High in Complex Carbohydrates	★★★★★★★★★
High in Dietary Fibre	★★★★★★★
Low in Saturated Fats	★★★★★★★★★★
High in Monounsaturated Fats	0
High in Polyunsaturated Fats	0
High in Iron	0
Low in Sodium	★★★★★★★★★★
High in Potassium	★★★★★★★
High in Calcium	0
High in Vitamin A	0
High in Vitamin C	★★★★
High in Vitamin B$_6$	★★★★★★★★
High in Folate	★★
Phytochemicals	★★★★★★

YAM

Scientific Name: *Dioscorea rotundata, cayenensis. alata.*

Origin and Background

The yam family was named after Dioscorides a Greek physician, who probably used the wild varieties as medicine. Yams are one of the oldest, nutritious, versatile, delicious staple foods. When yam is cut, slimy substances exude. These are soon oxidized and discolour the surface. Layers of dead, dry cells heal the surfaces when they are exposed to air. These dried cells protect the inner portion from drying out and guard against fungal attack. Despite this natural measure, many yams spoil very easily especially if they were not harvested and stored very carefully, and due to their high moisture (65–85%) content, they can be contaminated by viruses and moulds from the soil and in the air.

It is natural for the cut surface of some yams to discolour. Very rapid colour changes could mean that a virus is present or that the yam has a lot of polyphenols – the chemical substances which on exposure to air cause the colour changes. Sometimes these colour changes result in a bitter taste. Excesses of the chemical substances can be harmful.

The cut surface of mature yams can be prevented from darkening by covering with a piece of wax paper or thin plastic to keep out air. Another tip is to dip the peeled yam in a citric acid (lime, lemon or Seville orange juice) solution or other substance that retards oxidation. Some yams could have a purplish colour that may not be evenly distributed. This is a natural feature of those yams.

There are lots of chemicals (polyphenols) in immature (young) yams. From early times, people in the yam belt of Africa knew that there were poisonous substances in immature yams, and it was forbidden for many to eat them. Sometimes, people in the Caribbean reap and feed immature yams to their family, and some young children become very ill with vomiting and diarrhoea after eating. When these yams mature, they cause no ill effects on children or adults. Some people may experience a little itching or sting due to other chemicals called *oxalates* which may be in the yam. In the Caribbean, most of our mature yams are lower in oxalates than dasheen and coco (eddoe), two other common starchy roots.

Varieties

The best yams are short, compact, uniform in shape; smooth skinned and free of large roots often referred to as "hairs". The best yams are also resistant to insects and fungi in the ground and during storage. A good variety of yam has a long storage or shelf life before germination begins. Yams which have the above characteristics are good for cooking as well as processing into fries, chips, flour and pre-cooked flakes.

Some of the most familiar yams in the Caribbean are named after countries in the Caribbean. The St. Vincent yam is commonly called *Vinci* and Barbados (*Bauby, Bajan, Renta*) are two examples. Other yams are named according to their colour, taste, size, and heritage. There is yellow yam (*Afoo*), negro yam, white yam, chinese yam, yampie, mozzella and sweet yam. In Jamaica, there is another yam called Lucea, named after the capital of the parish of Hanover in which it grows very well. The four most important yams in the world are negro yam, yellow yam, white or lisbon yam and yampie. In the Caribbean, negro yams are best because there is usually little or no cut surface on the first bearing, that is of course if they were reaped and transported carefully so that there are no bruises and slits.

Health and Dietary Benefits

Yams provide a variety of health benefits. They contribute to boosting brain health, reducing inflammation, and improving blood sugar control. Nutritionally, yams are a good source of dietary fibre, potassium, manganese, copper, and antioxidants. Yams contain 65–85% water. Less water gives a finer structure and higher quality. Because of this high-water content, a larger amount of yam can be eaten to provide the same number of calories compared with other refined starches such as wheat flour and its products, or rice. Persons who must control their calorie intake, for example persons who are overweight and living with diabetes, and other overweight persons will benefit from substituting refined staples with yam or other (ground) provisions.

Yams are primarily a source of energy which is derived mostly from starch – a complex carbohydrate which is positive for promoting health. There is also some soluble fibre and little insoluble fibre or cellulose, so yams are digested very easily. Yams contain a small amount of protein, but when eaten with small amounts of meat, fish, cheese or eggs, the result is a nourishing meal. Yams are high in lysine, an essential amino acid, which is low in cereals. A mixture of yam flour with wheat flour, a meal with yam and dumplings or bread, and a smaller amount of animal protein makes for good total protein in that meal instead of yams alone.

Fresh yams are a good source of vitamin C which is vital in fighting infections such as colds and flu, and quick wound healing. Yams also help with anti-aging, strong bones, and healthy immune function. However, cooking results in loss of some of the vitamin C. Yams are also a source of the minerals, potassium, and phosphorus, but they are low in iron. Some people think that the purple fleshed yams are rich in iron but that is not so. The rich purple colour is caused by pigments called anthocyanins. Overall, the nutritive value of yams is very good.

The ease with which yams are digested makes them a suitable food for young children, especially if options of meat, fish, egg or cheese are also offered and a small amount of fat is added to give them the required calories with minimal bulk.

Preparation and Culinary Uses

Yam is versatile. When cooked, the flesh should be uniform in colour whether white, creamy, yellow or light purple. They should have a rich, smooth texture and they should not be bitter. Generally, yam is peeled and boiled as a starchy staple, but it can be baked, roasted, fried, grated, sliced, dried and ground into flour. It can also be prepared as chips or fries, mashed in pies or added to soups. Presentation can either be circles, wedges, diced, julienne or other shapes. Yams are sometimes roasted on charcoal, in hot wood ash or sand, scraped and served with its crisp, chewy skin. Roasted yam served with saltfish is a popular fast food on the roadside in sections of Jamaica. Citizens and visitors alike often stop to sample this treat and frequently take away some for later. Mashed yams make a delightful pie crust equalled only by mashed breadfruit.

Yam flour can be mixed with wheat flour at a higher percentage than other ground provision flours for domestic and commercial baked goods. This is possible because of the high protein content of the dried tuber and sticky nature of the starch. The traditional African way of preparing yam is peeling, boiling and beating in a mortar to stiff, sticky dough called Fufu which is rolled into small balls and served with stews and sauces. The balls are picked up with the fingers, dipped into the sauce or stew and eaten at festivals, celebrations, and daily meals. Yams are still regarded in Africa as a food of very high prestige and rightly so. It is a good principle to cherish and eat what we grow.

Other Uses

Yams can be used to make flour. The tuber is peeled and sliced. The slices are dried in the sun and then ground. If the slices are dried very well, the powdered yam will last for a very long time. With modern techniques, a higher-grade flour can be produced by hot air or solar drying.

RANK #3 – BREADFRUIT

Nutritional Criteria	Rating
High in Complex Carbohydrates	★★★★★★★★★☆
High in Dietary Fibre	★★★★★★★☆
Low in Saturated Fats	★★★★★★★★★☆
High in Monounsaturated Fats	0
High in Polyunsaturated Fats	0
High in Iron	0
Low in Sodium	★★★★★★★★★☆
High in Potassium	★★★★★★☆
High in Calcium	★★★☆
High in Vitamin A	0
High in Vitamin C	★★★☆
High in Vitamin B$_6$	★★★★★☆
High in Folate	0
Phytochemicals	★★★★★☆

BREADFRUIT

Scientific name: *Artocarpus altilis.*

Origin and Background

The breadfruit was first brought to the Caribbean in 1793 by a British explorer Captain William Bligh, as one of the cheap foods for feeding the slaves. This historical legacy, no doubt at one time, accounted for its own low status in the eyes of the Caribbean people, and it was many years before the breadfruit achieved widescale acceptability in the region. Today, however, some persons consider it as an exotic food.

Varieties

Varieties of the breadfruit are distinguished by the presence or absence of seeds, the shape and skin texture. Breadfruit varieties also differ in season of maturity, cooking quality and flavour.

The tree bears profusely for about eight months in the year, but much of the crop is wasted as it spoils easily because it ripens within two or three days of harvesting. Its storage life can be lengthened by placing it in the refrigerator. In the Caribbean, convenient and effective ways are being devised to store or preserve it on a large scale.

Despite its proven value over the 200 years since it was introduced to the region, the breadfruit's full potential is yet to be tapped. Processed breadfruit products developed in the Caribbean, include frozen dehydrated and canned slices as well as flour chips.

Health and Dietary Benefits

When compared with other single starchy foods eaten in Caribbean, the breadfruit can contribute to the diet appreciable amounts of energy, and the principal nutrients: protein, carbohydrates and dietary fibre. This Staple food can also make a valuable contribution to the dietary intake of calcium, magnesium, phosphorus, and potassium.

Breadfruit is rich in fibre and hence provides satiety without increasing the calorie intake. It is a healthy starchy option in low calorie diets. Regular intake of breadfruit is beneficial for proper bowel movement and intestinal functions because of the dietary fibre which also helps to reduce the "bad" cholesterol while increasing the amount of "good" cholesterol in the blood. Breadfruit is a rich source of potassium, iron, vitamins and minerals.

Preparation and Culinary Uses

In its fresh state, whether just mature, fully mature or ripe, the breadfruit can be used in many ways. Breadfruit can be boiled, baked, roasted, fried, pickled or prepared as chips. Breadfruit can also be frozen from one season to another by wrapping in wax paper and packaging it in plastic bags. Excess breadfruit can also be dried either in the sun or in the oven at 49°C (120°F). When used as a substitute for wheat flour, it is either grated or sliced, dried and ground. Breadfruit can also be added to mixtures to make dumplings, fritters, salads, porridge, cakes, muffins and puddings.

Other Uses

Every part of the breadfruit tree is valuable, including the leaves. For example, the tea of breadfruit leaves, which contain *camphoryl*, is used to lower blood pressure and treat diabetes. The leaves contain diuretic properties, which means that they gently aid the kidneys in elimination of excess sodium and fluid without depleting the body of essential minerals. In Jamaica, the sap is applied to contagious skin ailments to prevent spreading and promote healing. The sap can also be boiled to form a rubbery substance that is used to dress wounds.

RANK #4 – DASHEEN

Nutritional Criteria	Rating
High in Complex Carbohydrates	★★★★★★★★☆
High in Dietary Fibre	★★★★★★★☆
Low in Saturated Fats	★★★★★★★★★☆
High in Monounsaturated Fats	0
High in Polyunsaturated Fats	0
High in Iron	0
Low in Sodium	★★★★★★★★★☆
High in Potassium	★★★★★☆
High in Calcium	★★
High in Vitamin A	★★
High in Vitamin C	0
High in Vitamin B_6	★★★★★★★☆
High in Folate	★★
Phytochemicals	★★★★

DASHEEN

Scientific name: *Colocasia esculenta*
Other Common Names: Taro, Pacific Dasheen

Origin and Background

Dasheen or Taro is a tropical starchy root plant with a mildly sweet taste that has been cultivated for more than 6,000 years in China, Japan and the West Indies. It is the most widely cultivated species of several plants in the *Araceae* family. Dasheen is sometimes called a root vegetable but due to its starchy nature, this tuber is one of the foods in the Staple Food Group. All parts of this herbaceous crop, that is corm (tuber), large green leaves, and petioles (stalks) are edible. Dasheen plant parts contain oxalic acid which renders them acrid. Fortunately, however, this chemical is destroyed during cooking which makes it safe for human consumption.

Varieties

There are several varieties in the Caribbean *"Comme"* or *"Common"* is grown in Dominica. The flesh is light blue in colour after cooking. The *"White"* dasheen is cultivated mainly in St. Vincent and the Grenadines. This variety has many roots sprouting from the round corms that can be sometimes forked into two or four parts. Suckers, off shoots of the corm, grow into new plants. Other cultivars are the *"Noir"* that is grown in Dominica and the *"Pink"* dasheen in St. Vincent and the Grenadines.

Health and Dietary Benefits

Dasheen is a nutritious addition to both sweet and savory meals. It is a good source of various nutrients including carbohydrates, potassium and magnesium. It is an excellent source of dietary fibre, and resistant starch which are fermented by gut bacteria to form short-chain fatty acids, accounting for many of its health benefits. These include possible protection against colon cancer and inflammatory bowel disease, improved heart health, blood sugar levels, body weight and gut health. The high dietary fibre content contributes to reduced hunger thus providing extended satiety.

Dasheen also contains a variety of antioxidants and polyphenols that protect against free radical damage and potentially cancer. Its vitamin B_6 content is essential for the proper digestion and metabolism of food, as well as enzyme production and facilitation. It also contains vitamin E, an antioxidant involved with the reduction of the risk and effect of countless diseases associated with aging and other oxidative stressors. Dasheen is high in manganese which helps with iron absorption. Combined with the effects of vitamins E and B_6, manganese provides excellent support for blood and cardiovascular health. Good amounts of phosphorus and potassium are also found in dasheen, helping to maintain energy systems, and are linked to improved performance related to power and strength as well as proper health and quality of life in older adults.

Preparation and Culinary Uses

Dasheen should not be eaten raw as it contains compounds that may cause a stinging or burning sensation in the mouth. To prepare, wash the corm, trim the ends and peel away its outer tough hairy skin. Place its white interior flesh in cold water to remove sticky sap. Dasheen is generally prepared by boiling and can be sliced, cubed or mashed and converted into a savoury dish of choice. It may also be combined with other savoury or sweet tubers for variety.

Other Uses

The use of dasheen leaves with or without the stalks will be described in the vegetables section.

RANK #5 – BROWN RICE

Nutritional Criteria	Rating
High in Complex Carbohydrates	★★★★★★★☆
High in Dietary Fibre	★★★★★★★☆
Low in Saturated Fats	★★★★★★★★★☆
High in Monounsaturated Fats	0
High in Polyunsaturated Fats	0
High in Iron	★★
Low in Sodium	★★★★★★★★★★
High in Potassium	★★
High in Calcium	0
High in Vitamin A	0
High in Vitamin C	0
High in Vitamin B$_6$	★★★★
High in Folate	★★
Phytochemicals	★★★★★★

Note: Brown rice is not to be confused with Parboiled Rice.

BROWN RICE

Scientific name: *Oryza sativa*

Origin and Background

Rice is regarded as a first cultivated crop of Asia. Preserved rice grains were found in China around 3000 B.C. Rice is now a staple food of the Caribbean diet. The difference between brown and the other types of rice is more than the colour. A grain of rice has several layers. Only the outermost layer, the *hull*, is removed to produce brown rice. This process avoids the unnecessary loss of nutrients that occurs with further processing.

When brown rice is further milled to produce a whiter rice, it loses more nutrients because the bran and most of the germ layer is removed. The white rice that we buy undergoes further polishing and this removes the aleurone layer of the grain – a layer filled with health-supportive, essential fats. Because these fats, once exposed to air by the refining process, are highly susceptible to oxidation, this layer is removed to extend the shelf life of the product. The resulting white rice is simply a refined starch that is largely bereft of its original nutrients. It is important to note that brown rice is not the same as parboiled rice, a view held by many consumers.

Varieties

Brown rice like other forms of rice has many varieties each with its unique taste, appearance and texture after cooking. Long grain rice is long and slender. Medium grain rice is shorter and is a bit stickier after cooking. Short grain rice is short, and very sticky, mushy and absorbent after cooking. Parboiled rice is steamed prior to milling to seal in the nutrients and stabilize the starch on the surface of the grain. The varieties of milled, white or polished rice have the hull and the bran removed.

Health and Dietary Benefits

Rice in general is nutritious because it contains a range of nutrients and essential nutrition-related substances. Further, it is an excellent source of complex carbohydrates, one of the energy-producing nutrients that fuels muscles with glucose during activity and exercise and also feeds the brain to enhance its functioning. Rice also contains some protein, which the body needs for growth and repair of cells, tissues and muscles. Brown rice contributes minerals such as manganese, selenium and magnesium and is very low in sodium, has no cholesterol hence it is an excellent food to include in a sodium and/or cholesterol lowering diet. It is a good source of B vitamins, which are essential for metabolism in the release of energy from the food we eat and help the body to work efficiently. Brown rice is an excellent source of dietary fibre and thus can be used in controlled amounts by persons desirous of controlling their weight. It is also a good source of non-haem iron that requires some vitamin C to enhance its absorption.

Brown rice contains a small amount of rice bran oil. Soluble dietary fibre in brown rice has been shown to reduce high cholesterol levels, a plus against the development of atherosclerosis. Soluble fibre also helps to keep blood sugar levels under control, so brown rice is an excellent grain of choice for people living with diabetes. Fibre in brown rice can also help to protect against colon cancer because fibre binds to cancer-causing chemicals, keeping them away from the cells lining the colon. Magnesium, another nutrient for which brown rice is a good source, is helpful for reducing the severity of asthma, lowering high blood pressure, reducing the frequency of migraine headaches, and reducing the risk of heart attack and stroke. Eating foods high in insoluble fibre, such as brown rice, can help women avoid gallstones.

Preparation and Culinary Uses

Like other forms of rice, Brown rice is prepared in a variety of ways either as a separate dish or in combination with other ingredients to make a "one-pot meal". Some outstanding examples are pelau in Trinidad and Tobago; cook-up in Guyana and "ital rice and peas" a favourite part of Rastafarian dishes. Vegetable rice, fried rice, Spanish rice, jewelled rice, raisin rice, Christmas rice, channa rice are some other ways that rice is prepared. Various ethnic groups in the Caribbean also have unique ways of preparing rice. Generally, accompaniments may include seafood, meats, root crops/provisions, legumes, vegetable or other salads. Rice can also be used as stuffing or as a hot cereal/porridge.

Other Uses

Rice water – the water left over after any form of rice is cooked – has long been thought to promote stronger and more beautiful hair. It is also known as a skin treatment. Rice wine increases the collagen in the skin, which keeps the skin supple and helps prevent wrinkling. Rice wine also appears to have natural sunscreen properties.

RANK #6 – GREEN BANANA

Nutritional Criteria	Rating
High in Complex Carbohydrates	★★★★★★★☆
High in Dietary Fibre	★★★★★★★
Low in Saturated Fats	★★★★★★★★★☆
High in Monounsaturated Fats	0
High in Polyunsaturated Fats	0
High in Iron	0
Low in Sodium	★★★★★★★★★☆
High in Potassium	★★★★
High in Calcium	0
High in Vitamin A	0
High in Vitamin C	★★★★★☆
High in Vitamin B$_6$	★★★★★☆
High in Folate	0
Phytochemicals	★★★★

GREEN BANANA

Scientific name: *Musa acuminata, Musa balbisiana*
Other common names: Green Fig

Origin and Background

Bananas are believed to have originated about 10,000 years ago and may be the world's first fruit. Bananas were originally found in South-East Asia, mainly in India. They were brought west by Arab conquerors, moved from Asia Minor to Africa and finally carried to the New World by the first explorers and missionaries to the Caribbean.

The original bananas were small, like an adult finger, hence the name "banan", Arabic for finger. However, some believe the name may have come from a local language in West Africa. The sweet yellow banana is a mutant strain of the cooking/green banana, discovered in 1836 by Jamaican Jean Francois Poujot, who found that one of the banana trees on his plantation was bearing yellow fruit rather than green or red. Upon tasting the new discovery, he found it to be sweet in its raw state, without the need for cooking.

Varieties

It is widely believed that there are more than 1,000 types of bananas in the world, these are subdivided into 50 groups. Some countries refer to plantains as cooking bananas. In the Caribbean, cooking plantain and cooking banana are two different food items.

Health and Dietary Benefits

Bananas are nutrient dense being a good source of energy-producing complex carbohydrates, potassium, magnesium, vitamin B_6, the B group vitamins, vitamin C, dietary fibre and antioxidants and a reasonably good source of vitamin C. For these reasons, bananas provide numerous health benefits. They may boost digestive and heart health. They may even aid weight loss, as they are relatively low-calorie when used mindfully. They can help moderate blood sugar levels after meals and may reduce appetite by slowing stomach emptying. Because they provide sustaining energy, bananas are a favorite food for active children and adults, including athletes and sports enthusiasts.

Green bananas are generally considered healthy and give a feeling of fullness. In any form they are ideally suited for the gluten-free diet. Like the other starchy fruits, roots and tubers, its main nutrient is starch and, contrary to a widely held and popular belief, green banana provides little protein or iron. These nutrients are provided by whatever meat dish with which the green banana is often served.

Preparation and Culinary Uses

The green banana is a staple food which must be cooked, usually by boiling before eating. If you are not preparing green bananas after harvesting, they should be stored in the refrigerator to prevent them from turning ripe.

The banana can be used to make a variety of dishes. It can be grated, milk added and made into porridge, or used in other dishes such as salads, fritters, or as soused/pickled bananas. It can also be dried and made into flour, even replacing some of the wheat flour used to bake products. Commercially, it serves as the basis for an excellent snack food such as banana chips. It can also be used as a dessert or a breakfast item.

Example of a popular Caribbean dish is "run down" or "oil down", which consists of salted meats or fish (mackerel, shark or other fish of choice), coconut milk, green bananas, breadfruit or other starchy fruit, root or tuber, and greens (dasheen bush, callaloo, baghi, spinach). The versatility of green bananas makes them easy to add to your diet.

Other Uses

Banana skin /peel can be used in the kitchen as a cleaning product or in your beauty routine. It contains vitamin C and vitamin E and they also contain potassium, zinc, iron, and manganese. These nutrients can calm inflamed skin and reduce acne outbreaks. The potassium can help clean metal objects. A banana peel is also rich in enzymes which have a pulling action that will draw a foreign object to the surface of the skin which will make it much easier to grab with a pair of tweezers.

RANK #7 – FRESH CORN

Nutritional Criteria	Rating
High in Complex Carbohydrates	★★★★★☆
High in Dietary Fibre	★★★★★☆
Low in Saturated Fats	★★★★★★★★★☆
High in Monounsaturated Fats	0
High in Polyunsaturated Fats	0
High in Iron	0
Low in Sodium	★★★★★★★★★☆
High in Potassium	★★★☆
High in Calcium	0
High in Vitamin A	0
High in Vitamin C	★★★☆
High in Vitamin B$_6$	★★★☆
High in Folate	★★★☆
Phytochemicals	★★★★★☆

FRESH CORN

Scientific name: *Zea mays*
Other common names: Maize

Origin and Background

Although corn has been eaten all over the world for centuries, surprisingly, most of the corn grown is used to feed the animals we eat. Concerns have been raised about genetically modified (GMO) corn where scientists change the DNA in corn to make it more resistant to drought or insects, or to give it more nutrients. Importantly, fresh corn is not usually genetically modified. Non-GMO corn should be labelled as such.

Varieties

Sweet corn is the most popular and is primarily eaten from on the cob. It is extra sweet because it contains more natural sugars than other types of corn. Another favourite variety is *corn for popping*. This has a soft starchy centre surrounded by a very hard exterior shell. When it is heated, the natural moisture inside the kernel turns to steam that builds up enough pressure for the kernel to explode. *Flour corn* is primarily white. *Dent corn* is often used as livestock feed or to make processed foods. *Flint/Indian corn* is used for similar purposes as dent corn.

Health and Dietary Benefits

Corn is a good source of fibre, can help to lower blood cholesterol, regulate blood sugar and control weight. In addition, corn is a good source of vitamin C, magnesium, B vitamins, carotenoids, lutein and zeaxanthin. Carotenoids, lutein, and zeaxanthin have been shown to have antioxidative properties and are important in eye health. Vitamin C is important in cell repair, boosting immunity and has anti-aging properties. The B vitamins are important in energy metabolism. Magnesium is important for nerve conduction and muscle contraction.

Although corn contains beneficial nutrients, the health benefits are controversial. It is inferior to other cereals in nutritional value. It must therefore be complemented with other foods to make up for its niacin deficiency. Due to its starch content, consuming a large portion could spike blood sugar levels.

Preparation and Culinary Uses

Corn can be boiled, steamed, roasted, or grilled on the cob. The husk is sometimes kept intact when roasting and grilling. It makes a hearty addition to soups, stews, salads, and casseroles. Corn soup has become a favourite among Caribbean peoples at social gatherings. Its poor-quality gluten does not allow it to be used alone to make leavened bread. Popular by-products include corn flour, cornmeal, hominy or grits.

In some Caribbean countries, cornmeal is used to make porridge (hot cereal) and is sometimes added to flour to make dumplings. In Trinidad and Tobago, cornmeal is used to make a traditional Christmas food, pastelles, a steamed savoury cornmeal pie usually filled with seasoned meat, wrapped in banana leaf and steamed. Today, olives and raisins are added by many persons. It is said that pastelles are similar to Latin American tamales. Another traditional dish is, Paimee (pay-me), a sweet cornmeal pie filled with flavourful spices, raisins, coconut, sugar and rolled in a banana leaf and steamed to perfection. Corn is widely used in Latin American cuisine to make masa, a kind of dough used in such staple foods as tortillas and tamales.

Other Uses

Corn is used as livestock feed, as biofuel, and as raw material in industry. High fructose corn syrup is derived from corn syrup, which is made from extracting corn kernels and treating them with an enzyme to make a thick, viscous syrup. High fructose corn syrup differs from corn syrup in that some of the glucose in it is converted to fructose enzymatically, making it sweeter, whereas corn syrup is 100 percent glucose. High fructose corn syrup gets negative assessments because it is made up of fructose, a monosaccharide, that is sweeter than glucose and metabolized differently.

RANK #8 – SWEET POTATO

Nutritional Criteria	Rating
High in Complex Carbohydrates	☆☆☆☆☆☆
High in Dietary Fibre	☆☆☆☆☆☆
Low in Saturated Fats	☆☆☆☆☆☆☆☆☆
High in Monounsaturated Fats	0
High in Polyunsaturated Fats	0
High in Iron	0
Low in Sodium	☆☆☆☆☆☆☆☆☆☆
High in Potassium	☆☆☆
High in Calcium	0
High in Vitamin A	☆☆☆☆☆☆☆
High in Vitamin C	☆☆
High in Vitamin B$_6$	☆☆
High in Folate	0
Phytochemicals	☆☆☆☆

SWEET POTATO

Scientific name: *Ipomoea batatas.*

Origin and Background

Sweet potatoes are native to Central America and are one of the oldest root crops known to man. They have been consumed since prehistoric times as demonstrated by sweet potato relics that have been discovered in Peruvian caves dating back 10,000 years. In 1492, Christopher Columbus brought sweet potatoes to Europe after his first voyage to the New World. By the 16th century, they were brought to the Philippines by Spanish explorers and to Africa, India, Indonesia and southern Asia by the Portuguese. Around this same time, sweet potatoes began to be cultivated in the southern United States, where they remain as a staple food in the traditional cuisine and known as yam.

Varieties

Sweet potatoes are grouped into two categories depending upon the texture after cooking. One type is firm, dry, and mealy, while the other is soft and moist. Both types have a starchy but sweet taste with different varieties having different unique tastes. Depending upon the variety, of which there are about 400, the edible portion may be either white, yellow or orange, and its thin skin may either be white, yellow, orange, red or purple. Some of this root crop is shaped like an Irish potato, or are oval-shaped, circular or blocky with rounded ends, while others are longer with tapered ends.

Health and Dietary Benefits

The versatile sweet potato is ideal fare for the health-conscious food consumer. With the ever-growing interest in health and natural foods, the sweet potato has a place all year around in the diet for most persons, including infants from about 6 months old. Sweet potatoes are among the richest sources of potassium. Because of their high potassium content, they are contraindicated for persons with renal failure, unless they are leached.

Sweet potato has significant antioxidant properties due to the presence of beta-carotene, and vitamin C, very powerful antioxidants that work in the body to eliminate free radicals which damage cells and cell membranes, and are associated with the development of conditions like atherosclerosis, diabetic heart disease, and colon cancer.

They are also a good source of dietary fibre, which can lower the risk for diverticulosis, colon and rectal cancer, heart disease, diabetes and obesity. Some of the blood sugar regulatory properties of sweet potato may be due to the high concentration of carotenoids. Physiological levels, as well as dietary intake of carotenoids, may be inversely associated with insulin resistance and high blood sugar levels. People who are prone to constipation should eat sweet potatoes frequently because the insoluble dietary fibre stimulates intestinal peristalsis and hence facilitates defecation.

Sweet potatoes contain beta-carotene which, once consumed, is converted into vitamin A. This vitamin helps the skin to make sebum which is oily and helps to promote a healthy scalp. It is rich in pantothenic acid, which is known to moisturize when topically applied to the skin and increases skin integrity.

Preparation and Culinary Uses

Before cooking, sweet potato should be rinsed and scrubbed under cool water to remove any dirt or impurities from the skin. How you cut sweet potatoes largely depends on how you intend to cook them – they can be sliced into wedges, cubes, batons, medallions or left whole.

Sweet potato blends with herbs, spices and flavorings producing delicious dishes of all types, from baby foods to main dishes, casseroles, salads and breads. Sweet potatoes add valuable, appetizing nutrients and colour to any meal. An attractive and tasty dessert is sweet potato pie. Sliced sweet potato can be dusted with a blend of dried herbs if desired and deep-fried to make a crispy and tasty snack. Sweet potatoes can be steamed, sliced and sun-dried into a dry food for prolonged storage. They can also be roasted unpeeled. A welcome addition especially to holiday menus can be candied sweet potatoes or cinnamon-baked sweet potatoes. In short, sweet potatoes can be boiled, baked, roasted, grilled, mashed, fried, made into noodles, a cold salad like Irish potato salad or added to one-pot meal soups, among others.

RANK #9 – CASSAVA

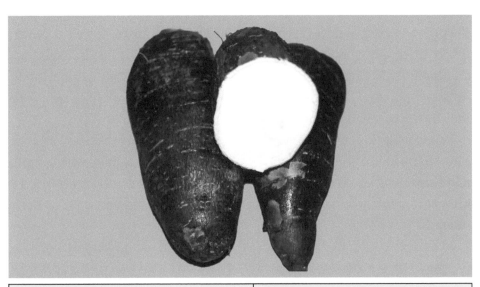

Nutritional Criteria	Rating
High in Complex Carbohydrates	☆☆☆☆☆☆☆
High in Dietary Fibre	☆☆☆☆☆☆
Low in Saturated Fats	☆☆☆☆☆☆☆☆☆
High in Monounsaturated Fats	0
High in Polyunsaturated Fats	0
High in Iron	0
Low in Sodium	☆☆☆☆☆☆☆☆☆☆
High in Potassium	☆☆
High in Calcium	☆
High in Vitamin A	0
High in Vitamin C	☆☆☆☆☆☆
High in Vitamin B$_6$	☆☆
High in Folate	☆☆
Phytochemicals	☆☆

CASSAVA

Scientific name: *Manihot esculenta*
Other common names: Manioc, Yuca

Origin and Background

Cassava originated in Brazil and Paraguay. Today, this root crop is widely diffused in the Caribbean region. In many parts of the world it is extensively cultivated as an annual crop for its edible starchy tuberous root. In the Caribbean it is a largely untapped resource as it produces an extremely large amount of food calories per cultivated area compared with other crop plants.

The chemical composition of cassava varies in different parts of the plant, and according to variety, location, age, method of analysis, and environmental conditions. Cassavas grown during a drought are especially high in toxins, which is a concern when the leaching process is not complete. Fresh tubers do not keep long but may be sliced and dried in the sun, with or without parboiling. The latter enhances the keeping quality allowing it to be stored for several months. Within recent times, cassava has been made available all year round because it is amenable to processing, particularly freezing.

Varieties

The root contains free and bound *cyanogenic glucosides (HCN)* which are converted to cyanide in the presence of linamarase, a naturally occurring enzyme in cassava. In the past, cassava was categorized as either sweet or bitter, indicating the absence or presence of toxic levels of cyanogenic glucosides. The so-called "sweet" (actually "not bitter") cultivars can produce as little as 20 mg of HCN (hydrogen cyanide) per kg of fresh roots, while "bitter" ones may produce more than 50 times as much (1g/kg). All varieties may require special processing to decrease the level of cyanogenic glucosides.

Health and Dietary Benefits

Cassava roots are high in starch (carbohydrates), making it a good energy source. Although cassava roots are rich in calories, they are deficient in proteins, fat, and some of the minerals and vitamins. This means that foods from animals must be eaten to make a nutritionally balanced diet. Cassava is reasonably rich in vitamin C, but the thiamine, riboflavin, and niacin content are not as high. Large proportions of these nutrients may be lost during processing. All of this should be noted in cassava-processing to retain these nutrients as much as possible. Because of its high potassium content, cassava is generally not recommended, unless leached, for use by persons with renal failure who are required to restrict dietary potassium. In contrast, cassava leaves are a good source of protein if supplemented with the amino acid, methionine.

Preparation and Culinary Uses

The root can be made into a variety of dishes. The soft-boiled root has a delicate flavour and can replace boiled potatoes in many uses: as an accompaniment to fish or meat dishes, or deep-fried, made into fufu (a thick paste made by peeling and cutting the boiled roots and pounding in a wooden mortar), dumplings, bread, cereal (farinha/farine), oil down/run down, salad, soups, and stews, Cassava flour can also replace wheat flour, and used by persons who are allergic to or cannot tolerate wheat, oats, rye or barley.

Cassava is also used for making *tapioca* – a common by-product produced by gently heating washed and clean starch on hot iron plates which partly cooks it and causes agglutination into small round pellets. This product can be used as a cereal or made into a dessert. Tapioca can also be used to make gluten-free bread.

Another much-used by product is *cassareep,* the finished dark-coloured concentrated product of boiled latex (milky fluid) and extracted juice. Cassareep is used in sauces and is a constituent of West Indian dishes, especially Guyanese pepper-pot.

RANK #10 – COCO

Nutritional Criteria	Rating
High in Complex Carbohydrates	★★★★★★
High in Dietary Fibre	★★★★★★
Low in Saturated Fats	★★★★★★★★★☆
High in Monounsaturated Fats	0
High in Polyunsaturated Fats	0
High in Iron	★★
Low in Sodium	★★★★★★★★★★
High in Potassium	★★★★★
High in Calcium	0
High in Vitamin A	0
High in Vitamin C	★★
High in Vitamin B$_6$	★★★★★★
High in Folate	0
Phytochemicals	★★

COCO

Scientific name: *Xanthosoma sagittifolium*
Other Common Names: Yautia, New Cocoyam, Tannia, Eddo.

Origin and Background

Coco is native to the Northern part of South America and the Caribbean. It is now a valued food crop in Florida (USA), Western Africa, parts of Egypt, India, and Oceania.

Varieties

Common varieties are generally red, white and yellow. In the English-speaking Caribbean, the varieties are South Dade White, Bruce and Rabess which are white-fleshed. Vinola and Jamaique are purple- to pink-fleshed.

Health and Dietary Benefits

Coco, a starchy tuber, comprises of slow digesting complex carbohydrates; and together with moderate amounts of dietary fibre, helps to regulate blood sugar levels. Yellow-fleshed coco and young, tender leaves have significant levels of phenolic flavonoid pigment antioxidants such as *ß-carotenes, and cryptoxanthin* along with vitamin-A. It also contains some of the vital B-complex group of vitamins such as pyridoxine folates, riboflavin, pantothenic acid, and thiamin. The corms provide some of the essential minerals like iron, zinc, magnesium, copper and manganese. Besides, the root has good amounts of potassium which is an essential component of cell and body fluids that help regulate heart rate and blood pressure. It does not contain gluten hence it is a good food source for people who are living with gluten-sensitive malabsorption diseases.

Preparation and Culinary Uses

This tuber must be washed, peeled, and cooked before it is eaten. It should not be eaten raw. Oxalates are the bitter, acrid substances found in coco cormels, which give astringent and burning sensation when eaten raw. Cooking eliminates these compounds and makes it safe for consumption. Adequate intake of water is recommended to flush out any absorbed oxalates in the cooked form. Cooked coco can be sliced, cubed or mashed with milk, and olive oil to make a tasty side dish. A choice of dried herbs or fresh seasonings can be added for added flavour. Coco is a natural thickener and can be added to soups and stews.

Other Uses

The young, unfurled leaves of some varieties can be eaten as steamed leafy vegetables or used in soups and stews.

Staples / Nutritional Criteria	Green Plantain (1)	Yam (2)	Breadfruit (3)	Dasheen (4)	Brown Rice (5)	Green Banana (6)	Fresh Corn (7)	Sweet Potato (8)	Cassava (9)	Coco (10)
High in Complex Carbohydrates	9	9	9	9	8	8	6	6	7	6
High in Dietary Fibre	8	8	8	8	8	8	6	6	6	6
Low in Saturated Fats	10	10	10	10	10	10	10	10	10	10
High in Monounsaturated Fats	0	0	0	0	0	0	0	0	0	0
High in Polyunsaturated Fats	0	0	0	0	0	0	0	0	0	0
High in Iron	0	0	0	0	2	0	0	0	0	2
Low in Sodium	10	10	10	10	10	10	10	10	10	10
High in Potassium	8	8	8	6	2	4	4	3	2	6
High in Calcium	0	0	4	2	0	0	0	0	1	0
High in Vitamin A	6	0	0	0	0	0	0	8	0	0
High in Vitamin C	6	4	4	2	4	6	4	2	6	2
High in Vitamin B$_6$	8	8	6	8	2	6	4	2	2	6
High in Folate	2	2	0	2	2	0	4	0	2	0
Phytochemicals	4	6	6	4	6	4	6	4	2	2

Summary of Ratings

BIBLIOGRAPHY

Holdip, J. (2006). *Common Caribbean Foods and Your Health* – Part 1. *Cajanus* Vol 39, No. 1.

Liu. S., Willett, W.C., Manson, J.E., Hu F.B., Rosne,r B. & Colditz, G. (2003). Relation between changes in intakes of dietary fibre and grain products and changes in weight and development of obesity among middle-aged women. *American Journal of Clinical Nutrition* 2003: 78 920-7.

McKeown, N.M, Saltzman, E., Meigs. J.B, Wilson, P.W.F., Liu, S. & Jacques, P.F. (2004) Carbohydrate nutrition, Insulin resistance and the prevalence of the Metabolic Syndromein the Framingham Offspring Cohort. *Diabetes Care* 2004, vol 27, 538–546.

Montagnac, J., Davis, C. & Tanumihardjo, S. (2009). Nutritional Value of Cassava for Use as a Staple Food and Recent Advances for Improvement. *Comprehensive Reviews in Food Science and Food Safety.* 8. 181–194. 10.1111/j.1541-4337.2009.00077.x.

Osborne, A. (2012). 10 *Things You Can Do with This Dinner Insurance.* Retrieved from http://www.dvo.com/newsletter/weekly/2012/04-27-369/dinner-insurance.html

Othman, R., 2 Kammona, S., 2 Jaswir, I., 2 Jamal, P. and 1 Mohd Hatta, F.A. (2017). Influence of growing location, harvesting season and post-harvest storage time on carotenoid biosynthesis in orange sweet potato (Ipomoea batatas) tuber flesh. *International Food Research Journal* 24(Suppl): S488-S495

Robin, Gregory C.,(2008). Commercial dasheen (Colocasia esculenta (L.) Schott var. esculenta) production and post-harvest protocol for the OECS, Caribbean Agricultural Research and Development Institute.

Wallace, A. (2006). Caribbean Foods. Retrieved from https://www.scribd.com/document/216830241/Caribbean-FOODS

CHAPTER 2 FRUITS

Fruits are the products from flowers. They are succulent, fleshy, or pulpy, often juicy, and usually sweet with fragrant, aromatic flavours. The Caribbean region is bountiful with a variety of fruits and they are extremely beneficial for maintaining health and preventing disease.

Fruits are generally good sources of calories due to their natural sugar content. They are often excellent sources of insoluble dietary fibre. These dietary fibres cannot be digested by humans but they are useful for managing many intestinal disorders such as irritable bowel syndrome, colon polyps/cancer, diverticulosis, haemorrhoids, constipation and diarrhoea. Fruits are generally rich in pectins – which are soluble fibres. These soluble fibres have been identified as having a role in controlling diabetes and cholesterol.

Fruits grown in the Caribbean are a powerhouse of vitamins and minerals when compared with the imported selections. Fruits can be used as attractive appetizers, complement a delicious meal or as palatable snacks. Fruits are seasonal and the prices will vary, but availability of a wide range of fruits throughout the year is not an issue.

Fruits are very nutritious and beneficial for all age groups, unless contraindicated for medical reasons. Children in particular, should be offered fruits and encouraged to eat them daily instead of more attractive but less nutritious commercial snacks.

RANK #1 – GUAVA

Nutritional Criteria	Rating
High in Complex Carbohydrates	★ ★
High in Dietary Fibre	★ ★ ★ ★ ★ ★ ★ ☆
Low in Saturated Fats	★ ★ ★ ★ ★ ★ ★ ★ ★ ★
High in Monounsaturated Fats	0
High in Polyunsaturated Fats	0
High in Iron	0
Low in Sodium	★ ★ ★ ★ ★ ★ ★ ★ ★ ☆
High in Potassium	★ ★ ★ ★ ★ ☆
High in Calcium	0
High in Vitamin A	★ ★
High in Vitamin C	★ ★ ★ ★ ★ ★ ★ ★ ★ ☆
High in Vitamin B$_6$	★ ★ ★ ☆
High in Folate	★ ★ ★ ☆
Phytochemicals	★ ★ ★ ★ ★ ☆

GUAVA

Scientific Name: *Psidium guajava*

Other Common Names: Lemon guava, apple guava, guayava, gougavé, goyave

Origin and Background

The term "guava" appears to have been derived from Arawak *guayabo* "guava tree", via the Spanish *guayaba*. Although originating in Latin America it has extended throughout tropical America and the Caribbean.

Varieties

The most frequently eaten variety that is often simply referred to as "the guava", is the apple guava (*Psidium guajava*).

Health and Dietary Benefits

Vitamin C content of guavas is high. A single fruit has about four times the amount as an orange. The dietary fibre content is also very good. The level of folic acid is good. Guava can be an excellent addition to the diet because it has a generally broad, low-calorie profile and other essential nutrients. Both the guava fruit and leaf extracts may boost your heart health, digestion, and immune system, in addition to other benefits.

Preparation and Culinary Uses

In many countries, guava is eaten raw sometimes with a pinch of salt and pepper. Guava drink is popular in many countries. The fruit is also often included in fruit salads. Because of its high level of pectin, guavas are extensively used to make candies, preserves, jellies, jams, guava cheese (a chewy fudge-like, melt-in-the mouth sweet), Brazilian goiabada and Colombian and Venezuelan bocadillo, and marmalade.

Guava is used in many ways. In some countries ripe guava is used in cooking and in others, it is a snack. In Asia, guava is commonly eaten with sweet and sour dried plum powder mixtures. Other countries have guava used as a beverage, in punch, and the juice is often used in culinary sauces, ales, candies, dried snacks, fruit bars, and desserts or an alcoholic beverage.

Other Uses

Since the 1950s, guavas particularly the leaves, have been studied for their constituents, potential biological properties, and history in folk medicine. Guava leaf extracts are taken as dietary supplements. Guava seed oil is possibly used for cosmetic products.

RANK #2 – CANTALOUPE

Nutritional Criteria	Rating
High in Complex Carbohydrates	★★
High in Dietary Fibre	★★★★
Low in Saturated Fats	★★★★★★★★★★
High in Monounsaturated Fats	0
High in Polyunsaturated Fats	0
High in Iron	0
Low in Sodium	★★★★★★★★★★
High in Potassium	★★★★
High in Calcium	0
High in Vitamin A	★★★★★★★★
High in Vitamin C	★★★★★★★★
High in Vitamin B$_6$	★★
High in Folate	★★
Phytochemicals	★★★★★★

CANTALOUPE

Scientific Name: *Cucumis melo* L.

Other Common Names: Rock melon, sweet melon, muskmelon, mushmelon

Origin and Background

The name *cantaloupe* came from the French *cantaloup* and Italian *Cantalupo*. However, the cantaloupe most likely originated in a region from South Asia to Africa. It later became a commercial crop in the United States. There are now cantaloupe farms in the Caribbean.

The fruit is a round melon with firm, orange, moderately sweet flesh. In-season cantaloupes have the brightest flesh colour and the sweetest and juiciest flavour. Off-season cantaloupes tend to be firmer with less flavour and can even be bland.

Varieties

The European cantaloupe is lightly ribbed with a sweet and flavourful flesh and a grey-green skin that looks quite different from that of the North American cantaloupe which has a "net-like" (reticulated) peel and is common in the United States, Mexico, the Caribbean, and some parts of Canada.

Health and Dietary Benefits

Fresh cantaloupe is a rich source of vitamin C and vitamin A. The fibre, potassium, vitamins and choline in cantaloupe all support heart health, help to control blood pressure, lower LDL cholesterol, and prevent constipation. Cantaloupe has many antioxidant and anti-inflammatory nutrients. It is relatively low in polyphenols, but it still provides important amounts because it is eaten in larger quantities than other fruits. Cantaloupe is low in calories yet packed with essential nutrients that help lower your risk for certain diseases. It also helps to keep the skin and hair healthy.

Preparation and Culinary Uses

Cantaloupe is generally cut as desired and eaten fresh. Because the surface of a cantaloupe can contain harmful bacteria, in particular *Salmonella*, it is recommended to wash and scrub a melon thoroughly before cutting and consuming. The fruit should be refrigerated after cutting and consumed in less than three days to prevent risk of *Salmonella* or other bacterial pathogens.

Cantaloupe is also used as a salad, or as a dessert with ice cream or custard. Melon pieces wrapped in prosciutto are a familiar antipasto. The seeds are edible and may be dried for use as a snack.

Other Uses

The raw seeds of cantaloupe are hard and not very tasty. Roasting the seeds with vegetable oil and spices improves the texture and produces a delicious taste. Both the fruit and the raw seeds can be blended with water then filtered to make a milk.

RANK #3 – PAPAYA

Nutritional Criteria	Rating
High in Complex Carbohydrates	★★
High in Dietary Fibre	★★★★★★★
Low in Saturated Fats	★★★★★★★★★
High in Monounsaturated Fats	0
High in Polyunsaturated Fats	0
High in Iron	0
Low in Sodium	★★★★★★★★★
High in Potassium	★★★★
High in Calcium	0
High in Vitamin A	★★★★★★★
High in Vitamin C	★★★★★★★★★
High in Vitamin B$_6$	0
High in Folate	★★
Phytochemicals	★★★★★★★

PAPAYA

Scientific Name: *Carica papaya*
Other Name: Pawpaw, Popoy

Origin and Background

The papaya is the fruit of the plant *Carica papaya*. It is thought to be indigenous to the West Indies and northern South America. The common name comes from the Taíno word *papáia* that was changed in Spanish to papaya, the word most used worldwide, with some changes. It was carried by the Spanish to Manila in the mid-1500s. From there it went to Malacca then India and reached Hawaii in 1800–1820s.

Varieties

Hawaiian and Mexican papaya are the two main varieties. In supermarkets, the common papaya is the Hawaiian variety which are more pear-shaped and have a yellow skin when ripe. The flesh is golden yellow or reddish-orange. The Mexican papayas are larger and have a rose-coloured flesh with a sweet flavor. In general, papaya has a unique taste that many people love. The skin of the fruit is thin and tough and is not eaten because it is too bitter. Firstly, the skin is green, but it changes to yellow in ripe ready-to-eat fruits. In a ripe fruit, the pulp is yellow, orange, pink, and even light red. Inside the fruit, there are many small black seeds.

Health and Dietary Benefits

Papaya is high in vitamins C and A, as well as fibre. The very high levels of carotenoids can help reduce inflammation. Papaya has powerful antioxidants like lycopene which may reduce the risk of many diseases such as heart disease and cancer. It may also defend against the visible signs of aging, helping your skin remain smooth and youthful.

Preparation and Culinary Uses

When papaya is ripe it can be eaten raw. After removing the skin and seeds, they are sometimes cut in small pieces and mixed with other fruits for a fruit salad. In tropical regions, it is very popular to make papaya juice, after peeling and removing the seeds. This juice can be mixed with milk to make smoothies. Unripe papaya should be cooked before eating – especially during pregnancy, as the unripe fruit is high in latex, which can stimulate contractions. Often, unripe papaya is cut in pieces and cooked with sugar and eaten as a sweet/candy or dessert.

Other Uses

Unripe papayas can be used as a meat tenderizer due to the presence of several enzymes. Papaya is also used as a beer stabilising agent.

RANK #4 – MANGO

Nutritional Criteria	Rating
High in Complex Carbohydrates	☆☆☆☆
High in Dietary Fibre	☆☆☆☆
Low in Saturated Fats	☆☆☆☆☆☆☆☆☆☆
High in Monounsaturated Fats	0
High in Polyunsaturated Fats	0
High in Iron	0
Low in Sodium	☆☆☆☆☆☆☆☆☆☆
High in Potassium	☆☆☆☆
High in Calcium	0
High in Vitamin A	☆☆☆☆☆☆☆☆
High in Vitamin C	☆☆☆☆☆☆☆☆
High in Vitamin B$_6$	☆☆☆☆
High in Folate	0
Phytochemicals	☆☆☆☆☆☆☆☆

MANGO

Scientific Name: *Mangifera indica* L

Origin and Background

The word mango originated from the Malayalam word mangga and Portuguese manga during the spice trade period with South India in the 15th and 16th centuries. Spanish and Portuguese explorers of the 15th century brought mangoes to the Caribbean.

Varieties

There are over 100 different varieties in the Caribbean. Each mango has a different colour, name, aroma, texture, shape and flavour. Mango eating is popular for both delicious green and ripe fruits. Green mango is crisp and crunchy. Ripening allows the mango to develop to its fullest, sweet, vivid, tropical ambrosia. Mangoes are abundant and ripe for harvest in early to mid-summer, that is during May to July in the Caribbean. The skin of mature mangoes is usually dull and matted. As the mango ripens and sweetens, its skin colour becomes more spectacular. Pale green turns to sunset yellow, blush pink to deep purple, multi colours turn striking red blush and crimson with bright yellow backgrounds.

Health and Dietary Benefits

Mango is low in calories if consumed in small amounts. They are rich in vitamins, minerals and antioxidants and have been associated with many health benefits, including potential anticancer effects as well as improved immunity, digestive, eye, skin, and hair health. It should be noted that while mangoes are delicious they contain more sugar than many other fruits and should not be over consumed.

Preparation and Culinary Uses

Mangoes are eaten as fruit. Commonly the fruit is held firmly by the hand and the flesh is enjoyed, sometimes along with the skin. Alternatively, mangoes can be divided into three parts – two fleshy outer slices/faces, plus the seed/stone. The flesh can also be scooped out with a spoon, cut into cubes or any other desired shapes.

Mangoes are widely used in cuisine. Mangoes may be used to make juices, nectar, and as a flavoring and major ingredient in ice cream and sorbets.

Sour, unripe mangoes are used in chutneys, athanu, pickles, side dishes, or may be eaten raw as chow (with salt, pepper, and other fresh seasonings, chili, or soy sauce). A summer drink called *aam panna* comes from mangoes. Mango pulp made into jelly or cooked with red gram dhal and green chillies may be served with cooked rice. Mango lassi is popular throughout South Asia, prepared by mixing ripe mangoes or mango pulp with buttermilk and sugar. Green to half-ripe firm mangoes are also used to make curries.

Aamras is a popular thick juice made of mangoes with sugar or milk and is consumed with chapatis or pooris. Mango is also used in Andhra Pradesh to make dahl preparations. Gujaratis use mango to make chunda (a spicy, grated mango delicacy). Mangoes are used to make murabba (fruit preserves) a sweet, grated mango delicacy, and amchur (dried and powdered unripe mango) eaten as a snack. Curried mangoes are a favourite of East Indian cuisine in the Caribbean.

Other Uses

Dried mango skin and its seeds are also used in Ayurvedic medicines. Mango leaves are used to decorate doors and buildings at celebrations in India. Paisleys are also common to Iranian art.

RANK #5 – ORANGE

Nutritional Criteria	Rating
High in Complex Carbohydrates	★★
High in Dietary Fibre	★★★★
Low in Saturated Fats	★★★★★★★★★★
High in Monounsaturated Fats	0
High in Polyunsaturated Fats	0
High in Iron	0
Low in Sodium	★★★★★★★★★★
High in Potassium	★★★★
High in Calcium	★★
High in Vitamin A	★★
High in Vitamin C	★★★★★★★★★★
High in Vitamin B$_6$	★★
High in Folate	★★
Phytochemicals	★★★★★★

ORANGE

Scientific Name: *Citrus sinensis*
Other Common Name: Sweet Orange

Origin and Background

The orange belongs to the citrus family in the species *Citrus sinensis*. During the Age of Discovery, Portuguese, Spanish, and Dutch sailors planted citrus trees along trade routes to prevent scurvy. Orange trees were found to be the most cultivated fruit tree in the world, but they are widely grown in tropical and subtropical climates.

The flavour of oranges may vary from sweet to sour. Sweet oranges grow in a range of different sizes and shapes. The orange contains a number of distinct *carpels* (segments) inside, typically about ten. Each carpel is delimited by a membrane, with many juice-filled vesicles, and usually a few seeds (*pips*). When unripe, the fruit is green. The ripe fruit can range from bright orange to yellowish orange.

Varieties

The *Citrus sinensis* group is subdivided into four classes with distinct characteristics. The general characteristics for grading are colour, firmness, maturity, varietal characteristics, texture, and shape. Grade numbers are determined by the number of unsightly blemishes on the skin and firmness of the fruit that do not affect consumer safety.

Health and Dietary Benefits

Oranges are an excellent source of vitamin C, as well as a good source of several other vitamins, minerals, and antioxidants. They contain diverse phytochemicals, including carotenoids (beta-carotene, lutein and beta-cryptoxanthin), flavonoids (e.g. naringenin) and numerous volatile organic compounds producing orange aroma, including aldehydes, esters, terpenes, alcohols, and ketones. These are associated with boosting the immune system and fighting free radicals. Hence, they may lower the risk of heart disease and kidney stones.

Preparation and Culinary Uses

Oranges are commonly peeled and eaten fresh, squeezed for juice or the peel/outermost layer used for its zest when thinly grated. Marmalade preserves are traditionally made with Seville oranges, which are less sweet. All parts of the fruit are used: the pith and pips (separated and placed in a muslin bag) are boiled in a mixture of juice, slivered peel, sliced-up flesh, sugar, and water to extract their pectin, which helps the preserve to set. The dried peel can also be used to make tea.

Orange juice is traded internationally in the form of frozen, concentrated orange juice to reduce the volume used so that storage and transportation costs are lower.

Other Uses

Sweet orange oil is a by-product of the juice industry produced by pressing the peel. It is used for flavoring food and drinks. Sweet orange oil is also used in the perfume industry and aromatherapy for its fragrance. It is also used in detergents and hand cleansers. Orange peel is used by gardeners as a slug repellent. Orange juice is widely used as a preservative.

RANK #6 – RIPE BANANA

Nutritional Criteria	Rating
High in Complex Carbohydrates	★ ★
High in Dietary Fibre	★ ★ ★ ★
Low in Saturated Fats	★ ★ ★ ★ ★ ★ ★ ★ ★ ★
High in Monounsaturated Fats	0
High in Polyunsaturated Fats	0
High in Iron	0
Low in Sodium	★ ★ ★ ★ ★ ★ ★ ★ ★ ★
High in Potassium	★ ★ ★ ★ ★ ★
High in Calcium	0
High in Vitamin A	0
High in Vitamin C	★ ★ ★ ★ ★
High in Vitamin B$_6$	★ ★ ★ ★ ★ ★
High in Folate	0
Phytochemicals	★ ★ ★ ★

RIPE BANANA

Scientific Name: *Musa sapientum*
Other Common Name: Ripe Fig

Origin and Background

Grown in more than 150 countries, banana is an edible fruit, produced by several kinds of large herbaceous flowering plants in the genus *Musa*. Musa species are native to tropical Indomalaya and Australia and are likely to have been first domesticated in Papua New Guinea. They are grown in 135 countries. The development of banana into a major worldwide trade commodity has its roots in the nineteenth century. Most cultivated bananas are especially in the Americas and Europe. "Banana" usually refers to soft, sweet, dessert bananas, particularly those of the Cavendish group, which are the main exports from banana-growing countries. Jamaica was the first commercial producer of bananas in the Western Hemisphere. The country's export trade began in 1866.

The fruits grow in clusters hanging from the top of the plant. The edible soft flesh is covered with a skin/rind, which may be green, yellow, red, purple, or brown when ripe.

As the crop is perishable, timing is of utmost importance. Fruit must be cut within a week's time to meet a shipping load. At the boxing plant, the selected bananas are hung on a conveyor and removed by hand from the stalk. They are then placed in tanks of water for at least four minutes to wash off the latex and other impurities.

Varieties

There are more than 1,000 types of bananas in the world. They are subdivided into 50 groups. The fruit varies in size, colour, and firmness, but is usually elongated and curved.

The most common is the Cavendish, the one most frequently produced for export markets. These are the long yellow, slightly sweet bananas at supermarkets around the U.S. They vary from under-ripe green to perfectly ripe and still firm mellow yellow, to riper deep yellow with a brown spot or two, to super soft with browning. Ripe bananas generally last 3–5 days in the home. Some common varieties in the Caribbean are *Gros Michel, Lacatan, Sucrier/Sikiyea and Silk Fig.*

Health and Dietary Benefits

Ripe bananas are relatively low-calorie and nutrient dense. They are a good source of dietary fibre, vitamin C and B$_6$ and a rich source of potassium. They may therefore boost digestive and heart health due to their fibre and antioxidant content.

Preparation and Culinary Uses

Eaten as a fruit when ripe, the skin is peeled off before use. Other uses include desserts, punches/smoothies, bread, cake, pancake, and fritters. This fruit can also be mashed and served to infants from 6 months of age.

Other Uses

Banana skins are known to relieve itching from rashes and bug bites. The banana stem is used in cloth production. Rope can be made from the dried stalk. Bananas can be used as animal feed, helping to reduce imports.

RANK # 7 – SOURSOP

Nutritional Criteria	Rating
High in Complex Carbohydrates	★★
High in Dietary Fibre	★★★★
Low in Saturated Fats	★★★★★★★★★★
High in Monounsaturated Fats	0
High in Polyunsaturated Fats	0
High in Iron	0
Low in Sodium	★★★★★★★★★★
High in Potassium	★★★★
High in Calcium	0
High in Vitamin A	0
High in Vitamin C	★★★★★★★
High in Vitamin B$_6$	★★
High in Folate	0
Phytochemicals	★★★★★★

SOURSOP

Scientific Name: *Annona muricata*
Other Name: Graviola, Guyabano, Guanábana

Origin and Background

Soursop is a broadleaf, flowering, evergreen tree that can grow to about 30 feet (9.1 m) tall. The fruits are dark green and prickly. They are ovoid and can be up to 30 centimetres (12 in) long, with a moderately firm texture. The soursop is adaptable to areas of high humidity and relatively warm winters.

The exact origin of soursop is unknown, but it is native to the tropical regions of the Americas and the Caribbean. Soursop is widely cultivated across the world and its derivative products are consumed in many diverse countries like Mexico, Brazil, Venezuela, Colombia, and Fiji. When the fruit becomes dry it is no longer good for consumption. With aroma similar to pineapple, the flavour of the fruit has been described as a combination of strawberries and apple, and sour citrus, contrasting with an underlying creamy texture reminiscent of coconut or banana.

Varieties

Popular varieties are 'Morada' (Brazil), 'Cuban Fibreless' (Australia), 'Sirsak Ratu' (Java), and 'Bennett', common in Florida. The flesh is juicy, acid, whitish and aromatic.

Health and Dietary Benefits

The fruit contains significant amounts of vitamin C, vitamin B_1 and vitamin B_2. The flesh of the fruit consists of an edible, white pulp, some fibre, and a core of indigestible black seeds. It is high in antioxidants, which may help prevent cell damage and could lower the risk of chronic disease. See debate about soursop under "other uses" below.

Preparation and Culinary Uses

The pulp is also used to make fruit nectar, smoothies, fruit juice drinks, as well as candies, sorbets, and ice cream flavourings.

Other Uses

The Memorial Sloan-Kettering Cancer Center lists cancer treatment as one of the "purported uses" of soursop. According to Cancer Research UK,

"Many sites on the internet advertise and promote graviola capsules as a cancer cure, but none of them is supported by any reputable scientific cancer organisations" and "there is no evidence to show that graviola works as a cure for cancer". Consequently, they do not support its use as a treatment for cancer. The compound annonacin, which is contained in the fruit and seeds of soursop, is a potent neurotoxin associated with neurodegenerative disease, and research has suggested that a connection between consumption of soursop and atypical forms of Parkinson's disease due to high concentrations of annonacin is conceivable. Practitioners of herbal medicine use soursop fruit and graviola tree leaves to treat stomach ailments, fever, parasitic infections, hypertension, and rheumatism. The leaves are also used as a sedative.

RANK #8 – NASEBERRY

Nutritional Criteria	Rating
High in Complex Carbohydrates	★★
High in Dietary Fibre	★★★★★★
Low in Saturated Fats	★★★★★★★★★★
High in Monounsaturated Fats	0
High in Polyunsaturated Fats	0
High in Iron	★★
Low in Sodium	★★★★★★★★★
High in Potassium	★★★★
High in Calcium	0
High in Vitamin A	0
High in Vitamin C	★★★★★★★
High in Vitamin B$_6$	0
High in Folate	★★★★★★
Phytochemicals	★★★★

NASEBERRY

Scientific Name: *Manilkara zapota*
Other Name(s): Sapodilla, Sapota, or Chikoo, Mesple

Origin and Background

This is a long-lived, evergreen tree native to southern Mexico, Central America, and the Caribbean. It is considered a special fruit with a unique taste of apple, pear and cinnamon flavouring.

Varieties

There are several varieties of naseberry classified by their size, fruit shape, skin colour and texture. The typical fruit in the Caribbean is a large berry, 4–8 cm (1.6–3.1 in) in diameter. Inside, its flesh ranges from a pale yellow to an earthy brown colour with a grainy texture akin to that of a well-ripened pear.

Health and Dietary Benefits

Naseberry is a high-calorie fruit and an excellent source of dietary fibre. It is also a good source of minerals like potassium, copper, iron and vitamins like folate, niacin, and pantothenic acid. It is therefore a great immune booster. It also assists the digestive system and the absorption of important nutrients.

Preparation and Culinary Uses

The fruit is cut in half or quarters and eaten fresh by scooping out the flesh. **NOTE:** Don't eat naseberry seeds: inside the black seeds is a tiny hook that could stick in your throat. Once ripe, naseberry fruit should be eaten within a few days. Mature but *unripe* fruits must be kept at room temperature for 7 to 10 days to ripen. Firm, ripe naseberries can keep well for several days in the home refrigerator, and if set at 35°F, they can be kept for up to six weeks.

Other Uses

Acetone extracts of the seeds exhibited *in vitro* antibacterial effects against strains of *Pseudomonas oleovorans* and *Vibrio cholerae*. Compounds extracted from the leaves have shown anti-diabetic, antioxidant and hypo-cholesterolemic (cholesterol-lowering) effects in rats. Naseberry has also been used to make body lotion, which is reported to firm the skin and provide deep hydration for a soothing and comforting feeling.

RANK # 9 – PINEAPPLE

Nutritional Criteria	Rating
High in Complex Carbohydrates	★★
High in Dietary Fibre	★★★★
Low in Saturated Fats	★★★★★★★★★★
High in Monounsaturated Fats	0
High in Polyunsaturated Fats	0
High in Iron	0
Low in Sodium	★★★★★★★★★★
High in Potassium	★★
High in Calcium	0
High in Vitamin A	0
High in Vitamin C	★★★★★★★★★★
High in Vitamin B$_6$	★★
High in Folate	0
Phytochemicals	★★★★

PINEAPPLE

Scientific Name: *Ananas Comosus, Ananas*
Other Name(s): Pine, Piña, Zanana

Origin and Background

The original name of the fruit comes from the Tupi word *nanas*, meaning "excellent fruit". The plant is indigenous to South America and is said to originate from the area between southern Brazil and Paraguay. However, little is known about the origin of the domesticated pineapple. The Paraná–Paraguay River drainages are considered to be the place of origin of *A comosus*.

The natives of southern Brazil and Paraguay spread the pineapple throughout South America, and it eventually reached the Caribbean, Central America, and Mexico, where it was cultivated by the Mayas and the Aztecs. Columbus encountered the pineapple in 1493 on the leeward island, Guadeloupe. He called it Piña de Indes, meaning "pine of the Indians", and brought it back with him to Spain, thus making the pineapple the first bromeliad to be introduced by humans outside of the New World. "Pineapple was the fruit of colonialism" because the Portuguese, French, Dutch, and British all sought to establish pineapple plantations in the tropics of South America, Central America, and the Caribbean.

Bromelain is a mixture of proteolytic enzymes and is present in all parts of the pineapple plant. Bromelain is under preliminary research for a variety of clinical disorders, but to date has not been adequately defined for its effects in the human body. Care should be taken because Bromelain may be unsafe for some users, such as in pregnancy, allergies, or anticoagulation therapy.

After cleaning and slicing, a pineapple is sometimes canned in own juice or sugar syrup with added preservative. After harvesting a pineapple will become softer and juicier, but it will not become sweeter. This is because the pineapple sugar comes from the starches in the stem. Once that source is cut off, the pineapple cannot make more sugar on its own. The fruit itself is quite perishable and if it is stored at room temperature, it should be used within two days. However, if it is refrigerated, the time span extends to 5–7 days.

Varieties

There are more than 35 varieties of pineapples with four main classes: red spanish, queen, abacaxi, and smooth cayenne. Consumers believe Abacaxi and queen varieties are the most delicious. Red Spanish is orange-red and is the major variety grown in the Caribbean. Some buyers prefer the green fruit, others like the ripened or off-green variety. A plant growth regulator, Ethephon, is typically sprayed onto the fruit one week before harvest, developing ethylene, which turns the fruit golden yellow.

Health and Dietary Benefits

Pineapple is a rich source of manganese and vitamin C. It has been linked to health benefits such as a lower risk of cancer, improved immunity, relief of arthritis symptoms as well as improved digestion.

Preparation and Culinary Uses

Fresh pineapple is generally served in wedges or rings. Pineapple is also used in many other ways. It is added to fruit salad, pies, cakes, ice cream, yogurt, punches, and other desserts. It is an ingredient in most sweet and sour dishes and is used in many savoury dishes.

The flesh and juice of the pineapple are used in cuisines around the world. In many tropical countries, pineapple is prepared and sold on roadsides as a snack or can be flavoured with salt, hot pepper, and other fresh herbs to make pineapple chow. It is often used as garnish on hams and as fruit salad. In the Caribbean it is a common pizza topping and is an appetizing addition to hanburgers as well as bake and shark. Traditional dishes in Hawaii usually include pineapple. Crushed pineapple is often added to yogurt, jam, sweets, and ice cream. The juice of the pineapple is the main ingredient in cocktails such as the piña colada.

Other Uses

The long leaves of the 'Red Spanish' cultivar were the source of traditional piña fibres, an adaptation of the native weaving traditions. These were woven into lustrous lace-like fabrics usually decorated with intricate floral embroidery. The fabric was a luxury export from the Philippines during the Spanish colonial period and gained favour among European aristocracy in the 18th and 19th centuries.

RANK #10 – JUNE PLUM

Nutritional Criteria	Rating
High in Complex Carbohydrates	★★
High in Dietary Fibre	★★★★
Low in Saturated Fats	★★★★★★★★★★
High in Monounsaturated Fats	0
High in Polyunsaturated Fats	0
High in Iron	0
Low in Sodium	★★★★★★★★★★
High in Potassium	★★
High in Calcium	0
High in Vitamin A	0
High in Vitamin C	★★★★★★★★
High in Vitamin B$_6$	0
High in Folate	0
Phytochemicals	★★★★

JUNE PLUM

Scientific Name: *Spondias dulcis*
Other Name(s): Golden Apple, Pommecythere, Jew Plum; Mangotín; Jobo Indio; Kedondong and Buah Long Long

Origin and Background

Indigenous to Hawaii, the fruit was originally introduced to the Caribbean in 1782 when it was brought to Jamaica by Captain Bligh. It is craved for its succulent and sweet but tart ripe pulp which has a high nutritional value. Around the world it has many names, but common names in the Caribbean are June Plum (Jamaica) Golden Apple (Barbados and Guyana) and Pommecythere (Trinidad and Tobago).

Varieties

The June plum is a variety of plum which is different from other plums. It is oval shaped, has a thick skin and a tropical bouquet of flavors and aromas. It has a creamy coloured semi-acidic firm flesh with flavors of pineapple, mango, and apple. It has a fibrous or hairy seed. While unripe, the flesh is crisp and firm with a tart acidic taste, ideal for making chow. As it ripens, it turns yellow, becomes soft and develops the sweet taste and fragrant smell.

Health and Dietary Benefits

June plums are a good source of vitamin C, vitamin K and fibre. The antioxidants help with proper bodily functions. June plums are also linked to the relief of headaches, constipation.

Preparation and Culinary Uses

It is eaten as a snack, dessert or used as a fruit beverage. Both ripe and unripe fruits can be eaten raw. It is also often prepared by juicing, stewing with ginger and sugar, pickling with peppers and spices, or made into chow. The fruit can also make jellies, jams, and pickles. Select fruits that are free from blemishes, cuts, and bruises. Store at room temperature and consume as soon as possible.

Other Uses

June plum is reputed to eliminate dandruff. Apply the pulp into your scalp and massage gently before rinsing it off.

Fruits

Nutritional Criteria	Guava	Cantaloupe	Papaya	Mango	Orange	Ripe Banana	Soursop	Naseberry	Pineapple	June plum
	1	2	3	4	5	6	7	8	9	10
High in Complex Carbohydrates	2	2	2	4	2	2	2	2	2	2
High in Dietary Fibre	8	4	8	4	4	4	4	6	4	4
Low in Saturated Fats	10	10	10	10	10	10	10	10	10	10
High in Monounsaturated Fats	0	0	0	0	0	0	0	0	0	0
High in Polyunsaturated Fats	0	0	0	0	0	0	0	0	0	0
High in Iron	0	0	0	0	0	0	0	2	0	0
Low in Sodium	10	10	10	10	10	10	10	10	10	10
High in Potassium	6	4	4	4	4	6	4	4	2	2
High in Calcium	0	0	0	0	2	0	0	0	0	0
High in Vitamin A	2	8	8	8	2	0	0	0	0	0
High in Vitamin C	10	8	10	8	10	5	7	7	10	8
High in Vitamin B_6	4	2	0	4	2	6	2	0	2	0
High in Folate	4	6	8	8	6	4	0	6	0	0
Phytochemicals	6	6	8	8	6	4	6	4	4	4

Summary of Ratings

BIBLIOGRAPHY

Akanda, Md. Khokon & Mehjabin, Sanzia & Uzzaman, Shakib & Parvez, Masud. (2018). A short review on a Nutritional Fruit: Guava. *Toxicology Research*. 1. 1–8.

Aravind. G, Debjit Bhowmik, Duraivel. S , Harish. G (2013). Traditional and Medicinal Uses of Carica papaya. *Journal of Medicinal Plants Studies,* Volume :1, Issue :1

Badrie, N & Schauss, A. (2010). Soursop (Annona muricata L.): Composition, nutritional value, medicinal uses, and toxicology. 10.1016/B978-0-12-374628-3.00039-6.

Barbalho, Sandra & Machado, Flávia. (2012). Psidium Guajava (Guava): A Plant of Multipurpose Medicinal Applications. *Medicinal & Aromatic Plants*. 01. 10.4172/2167-0412.1000104

Beaulieu, J., Perkins, P., & Siddiq, M. (2012). Watermelon, Cantaloupe, and Honeydew. 10.1002/9781118324097.

Banana Retrieved from https://en.wikipedia.org/wiki/Banana

Banana production in the Caribbean. Retrieved from https://en.wikipedia.org/wiki/Banana_production_in_the_Caribbean

Bennett, S. (2020). Sapadilla- Foods that feed your sweet tooth. Retrieved from https://www.uncommoncaribbean.com/caribbean/taste-of-the-caribbean-sapodilla-fruit-that-feeds-your-sweet-tooth/

Carlier, J., d'Eeckenbrugge, G & Leitao, J (2007). Pineapple. 10.1007/978-3-540-34533-6_18.

Chandra, Ramesh & Kamle, Madhu & Bajpai, Anju. (2010). Guava. 10.13140/RG.2.1.3793.9042.

Chaudhary, Vipul & Kumar, Vivak & Sunil, Er & Shami, Vaishali & Singh, Kavindra & Kumar, Ratnesh & Kumar, Vikrant. (2019). Pineapple (Ananas cosmosus) product processing: A review. 8. 4642-4652.

Devi Prasad, P.V. (1986). Edible Fruits and Vegetables of the English-Speaking Caribbean, Caribbean Food and Nutrition Institute, Kingston, Jamaica.

Drhealthbenefits. (nd). 20 impressive Health Benefits of Golden Apple Fruit. Retrieved from https://drhealthbenefits.com/food-bevarages/fruits/health-benefits-golden-apple-fruit

Health benefits time. Sapodilla facts and health benefits. Retrieved from https://www.nutrition-and-you.com/sapodilla.html

Keita, K. (2017). Papa, papa, PAPAYA! Retrieved from https://www.thegardenisland.com/2007/07/04/news/papa-papa-papaya/

Laib, R. (2013). 20 Delicious Ways to Use Pineapple. Retrieved from https://www.google.com/search?q=culinary+uses+of+pineapple&rlz

Lo'ay, A. & Harbinson, Jeremy & Kooten, Olaf. (2005). General introduction: Mangoes. Wageningen Agricultural University Papers. 1–21.

Lpatenco, S. (2020). Types of Papaya Fruit. Retrieved from https://www.livestrong.com/article/516915-types-of-papaya-fruit/

Manilkara zapota. Retrieved from https://en.wikipedia.org/wiki/Manilkara_zapota

Milind, P. & Dev, C. (2012) Orange: Range of Benefits. *International Research Journal of Pharmacy* www.irjponline.com ISSN 2230–8407

Medical News Today. What to know about oranges Retrieved from https://www.medicalnewstoday.com/articles/272782.php

Medical News Today, (2019). Everything you need to know about cantaloupe. Retrieved from https://www.medicalnewstoday.com/articles/279176.php

Mishra R, Tiwari P, Srivastava M, Singh CS, Ghoshal S. A comprehensive review on Psidium guajava Linn (Amaratafalam). *International Journal of Ethnobiology & Ethnomedicine.* 2017 Apr 27 [last modified: 2017 May 1]. Edition 1.

Mohammed, M., Puran, B., Mohamed, M.S. Bridgemohan, R.S.H. & Mohammed, Z. (2017). Postharvest Physiology and Storage of Golden Apple (Spondias cytherea sonnerat or Spondias dulcis forst): A Review. *Journal of Food Processing & Technology.* 8. 10.4172/2157-7110.1000707.

Mohammed, M., Ahmad, S. H., Bakar, R. A., & Abdullah, T. L. (2011). Golden apple (spondias dulcis forst. syn. spondias cytherea sonn.). In Postharvest biology and technology of tropical and subtropical fruits (pp. 159-180e). Woodhead Publishing.

Nayar, N. (2010). The Bananas: Botany, Origin, Dispersal. 10.1002/9780470527238.ch2.

Orange fruits. Retrieved from https://en.wikipedia.org/wiki/Orange_(fruit)

Orange (fruit). Retrieved from https://www.en.w3ki.com/wiki/Orange_fruit

Parle, Milind & Gurditta, (2011). Basketful benefits of papaya. *International Research Journal of Pharmacy.* 2. 6–12.

Pineapple. Retrieved from https://en.wikipedia.org/wiki/Pineapple

Pua, Eng-Chong. (2007). Banana. 10.1007/978-3-540-49161-3_1.

Robert J. Lancashire,(1997) Papaya – pawpaw. Retrieved from http://wwwchem.uwimona.edu.jm/lectures/papaya.html

Slavin, J. L., & Lloyd, B. (2012). Health benefits of fruits and vegetables. Advances in nutrition (Bethesda, Md.), 3(4), 506–516. https://doi.org/10.3945/an.112.002154

Shah, K.A. & Patel, M.B. & Patel, R.J. & Parmar, P.K. (2010). Mangifera Indica (Mango). *Pharmacognosy reviews.* 4. 42–8. 10.4103/0973-7847.65325.

Soursop. Retrieved from https://en.wikipedia.org/wiki/Soursop

Teixeira da Silva, J., Rashid, Z., Nhut, D., Sivakumar, D., Gera, A., Souza Junior, M. & Tennant, P. (2007). Papaya (Carica papaya L.) Biology and Biotechnology. *Tree and Forestry Science and Biotechnology.* 1. 47–73.

The Caribbean Dictionary. Retrieved from http://wiwords.com/word/golden-apple

Yahia, Elhadi. (2014). Sapodilla and Related Fruits.

Wikipedia the free encyclopedia. Soursop. Retrieved from https://www.wikizero.com/en/Soursop

CHAPTER 3 | VEGETABLES

Vegetables are plants or parts of plants that can be used as food. Because of the high starch content, tubers and corn are categorized as Staples. Similarly, peas are placed with Legumes.

Vegetables make a massive contribution to the body's requirements for minerals, vitamins and dietary fibre. Many vegetables contain carotene which is converted into vitamin A in the body. Vitamin A is essential for normal growth and vitality, for healthy vision, healthy skin and for protection against diseases, especially of the respiratory tract. Several leafy vegetables contain riboflavin, a member of the vitamin B-complex family. This vitamin is essential for growth and general health of eyes, skin, nails, and hair. Vitamin C is contained in good amounts in several vegetables such as tomatoes and leafy vegetables like spinach, dasheen leaves, cabbage and callaloo. Vitamin C is essential for normal growth and maintenance of body tissues, especially those of the joints, bones, teeth, and gums, and for protection against infection. The highly soluble minerals like calcium, phosphorus, iron, magnesium, copper, and potassium contained in vegetables maintain the acid-base balance of the body tissues and help with the metabolism of proteins, fats, and carbohydrates. They also help the body to eliminate excess body water and salt. Two important minerals, calcium and iron, found in vegetables are especially useful. Calcium is essential for strong bones and teeth, and iron is essential for blood formation.

Vegetables also contribute both soluble and insoluble dietary fibre. The latter does not dissolve in water and is also referred to as roughage or bulk. Fibre includes cellulose, hemicellulose and lignin and is found in most vegetables. Fibre promotes the peristaltic or wavelike contractions that keep food moving through the intestines. Soluble fibre either swells or dissolves in water. Most foods of plant origin contain mixtures of soluble and insoluble fibres thus eating fruits and vegetables daily will provide this mixture.

Like fruits and wholegrain cereals, vegetables contain large amounts of antioxidant phytochemicals, which, together with vitamins and minerals, may exert protection against gastrointestinal cancers and cardiovascular diseases.

RANK #1 – CALLALOO

Nutritional Criteria	Rating
High in Complex Carbohydrates	0
High in Dietary Fibre	★★★★★★★★
Low in Saturated Fats	★★★★★★★★★
High in Monounsaturated Fats	0
High in Polyunsaturated Fats	0
High in Iron	★★★★★★★★
Low in Sodium	★★★★★★
High in Potassium	★★★★★★★★
High in Calcium	★★★★★★★
High in Vitamin A	★★★★★★★★★
High in Vitamin C	★★★★★★★★
High in Vitamin B$_6$	★★★★★★★★
High in Folate	★★★★★★★★
Phytochemicals	★★★★★★★★

CALLALOO

Scientific Name: *Amaranthus viridis*
Other Common Names: Calalloo, Calaloo or Kallaloo, Chorai bhagi

Origin and Background

Callaloo has been described as "hot-weather spinach" that originated from West Africa. It was used by enslaved Africans in the Caribbean and has become a popular vegetable dish. Callaloo varies in its preparation from Belize in the north to Guyana and Suriname in the south.

Varieties

The callaloo consists of about 60 varieties. In Jamaica alone there are three varieties of callaloo. Callaloo is a leafy, spinach-like vegetable. The variety of callaloo *Amaranthus viridis*, better known as Chinese spinach or Indian kale, should not be confused with the dish called callaloo, the main ingredient being the leaves of the dasheen plant (see rank #2 item) a favourite in the Eastern Caribbean islands as well as Trinidad and Tobago. In some of these islands can be found a similar vegetable called bhagi.

Health and Dietary Benefits

Callaloo leaves contribute limited calories but they are a good source of dietary fibre, iron and rich in minerals such as potassium, calcium, vitamins A, C, B_6 and folate, and phytochemicals. Vitamin C helps with boosting the immune system; B Vitamins help with mood and vitality, and Vitamin A is a great antioxidant. The potassium helps to lower or maintain blood pressure and regulate heartbeat. The calcium makes strong bones and teeth and aids in the clotting of blood. The fibre in callaloo helps to form bulk in the formation of faeces, makes a person feel less hungry after eating, slows the absorption of glucose in the cells, traps excess fat in the intestines and lowers LDL or "bad" cholesterol. The fibre also helps to prevent constipation and create an ideal environment for growth of probiotic bacteria thus boosting your immune system. Cooked callaloo provides more iron than raw callaloo. However, to help get the iron in the blood, callaloo should be consumed with fruits or vegetables high in vitamin C, such as, tomato, oranges or West Indian cherries. As a low-calorie vegetable, it is an excellent and healthy choice for almost everyone especially persons who are weight conscious.

Preparation and Culinary Uses

Callaloo is often steamed with added ingredients such as tomatoes, salt, peppers, onions, and scallions and eaten as a side dish with many meals. It can also be made into a soup or used as a filler in pies/patties/pastries. Different countries have added coconut milk, okra, conch, crab, meats, garlic, onion, among others to make their own distinctive flavor.

Other Uses

Some amaranth species are cultivated as leaf vegetables, pseudo-cereals, and ornamental plants.

RANK #2 – DASHEEN LEAVES

Nutritional Criteria	Rating
High in Complex Carbohydrates	0
High in Dietary Fibre	★ ★ ★ ★ ★ ★ ★ ☆
Low in Saturated Fats	★ ★ ★ ★ ★ ★ ★ ★ ★ ☆
High in Monounsaturated Fats	0
High in Polyunsaturated Fats	0
High in Iron	★ ★ ★ ★ ★ ★ ★ ★ ☆
Low in Sodium	★ ★ ★ ★ ★ ★ ★ ★ ★ ☆
High in Potassium	★ ★ ★ ★ ★ ★ ☆
High in Calcium	★ ★ ★ ★ ★ ★ ★ ☆
High in Vitamin A	★ ★ ★ ★ ★ ★ ★ ☆
High in Vitamin C	★ ★ ★ ★ ★ ★ ☆
High in Vitamin B$_6$	★ ★ ★ ☆
High in Folate	★ ★ ★ ★ ★ ★ ★ ☆
Phytochemicals	★ ★ ★ ★ ★ ★ ★ ☆

DASHEEN LEAVES

Scientific Name: *Colocasia esculenta*
Other Common Names: Dasheen Bush, Dasheen Bush Bhagi, Taro Leaves, Elephant Ears

Origin and Background

The Spanish brought the plant to the Americas and today leaves can be found in fresh markets across the world in Asia, Southeast Asia, Polynesia, the Cook Islands, the Caribbean, and in tropical Africa. The plant is perennial and can grow over two meters in height.

The dark green leaves are either small, medium or large in size, broad and heart-shaped or elephant ear-shaped. They average up to forty centimeters in length and twenty centimeters in width. The leaves are smooth on the surface and light green on the underside which has veins that branch out from the central stem. Both the veins and stem generally have a purple to red hue and are often variegated.

Varieties

Leaves are either rolled or opened flat, medium to large depending on the maturity of the crop.

Health and Dietary Benefits

Dasheen leaves are low in calories, but they are a good source of dietary fibre, iron and rich in minerals such as potassium, calcium, vitamins A, C, B_6 and folate, and phytochemicals. Vitamin C helps with boosting the immune system; B Vitamins help with mood and vitality, and Vitamin A is a great antioxidant.

As a low-calorie vegetable, it is an excellent and healthy choice for almost everyone especially persons who are weight conscious. The dietary fibre helps to prevent constipation and create a good environment for growth of probiotic bacteria thus boosting your immune system.

Preparation and Culinary Uses

The leaves and stalks must be cooked before consumption after thoroughly washing. The green leaves and stems are used generally to make a dish called callaloo, a favourite in the cuisine of Trinidad and Tobago and many of the other Caribbean countries. The dish known as Callaloo is a blend of dasheen/taro leaves and stems, okra, pumpkin, coconut milk or crème, herbs, margarine or butter, and optional: pickled cured beef or pork, crab, smoked turkey or chicken and hot pepper. The dasheen leaves and stalks can also be sautéed and used as a side dish or as an ingredient in pies/pastries, selected East Indian dishes, oil-down/run-down, or combined with rice (cook-up). Combining or converting this vegetable into dishes can negate the low caloric value.

Other Uses

Dasheen is also grown as an ornamental plant, often referred to as "elephant ears".

RANK #3 – SPINACH

Nutritional Criteria	Rating
High in Complex Carbohydrates	0
High in Dietary Fibre	✮✮✮✮✮✮✮✩
Low in Saturated Fats	✮✮✮✮✮✮✮✮✩
High in Monounsaturated Fats	0
High in Polyunsaturated Fats	0
High in Iron	✮✮✮✮✮✮✩
Low in Sodium	✮✮✮✮✮✮✩
High in Potassium	✮✮✮✮✮
High in Calcium	✮✮✮✩
High in Vitamin A	✮✮✮✮✮✮✩
High in Vitamin C	✮✮✮✮✮✮✩
High in Vitamin B_6	✮✮✮✮✮✮✩
High in Folate	✮✮✮✮✮✮✩
Phytochemicals	✮✮✮✮✮✮✩

SPINACH

Scientific Name: *Spinacia oleracea*
Other Common Names: Persian Greens

Origin and Background

Spinach is a leafy green flowering plant native to Central and Western Asia. Spinach cultivation is thought to have originated from ancient Persia, later spreading to Nepal, and by the seventh century, to China, where it's still called "Persian Greens". The Moors introduced it to Spain around the 11th century.

Varieties

There are three varieties of spinach – savoy, semi-savoy, and flat-leafed. Each of these varieties has their cultivars or sub-varieties. Savoy spinach boasts dark green curly leaves, having a slightly crunchy and crispy texture. Semi-savoy spinach is similar to savoy in that it has the same crisp texture and flavour but it is less crinkly than savoy and hence easier to clean. Flat-leafed spinach is different from the others because of its broad and flat-shaped green leaves that are easier to clean. This variety is the favorite among consumers.

Health and Dietary Benefits

Spinach is low in calories but packed with nutrients and antioxidants. It is a rich source of vitamin A, vitamin C, vitamin K, magnesium, manganese, iron, and folate. Spinach is also a good source of the B vitamins: riboflavin and vitamin B_6; vitamin E, calcium, potassium, and dietary fibre. Eating spinach may therefore benefit eye health, reduce oxidative stress, help prevent cancer, and reduce blood pressure levels.

Preparation and Culinary Uses

Spinach leaves are a common edible vegetable consumed either fresh, or after storage using preservation techniques by canning, freezing, or dehydration. It may be eaten cooked or raw, and the taste differs considerably. The high oxalate content may be reduced by steaming. Spinach is becoming more prevalent in the salad bar. Its versatility makes it easily adaptable in healthy vegetable drinks and smoothies, lightly sautéed as a stand-alone side dish, and added to soups.

RANK #4 – PAK CHOI

Nutritional Criteria	Rating
High in Complex Carbohydrates	0
High in Dietary Fibre	✮✮✮✮
Low in Saturated Fats	✮✮✮✮✮✮✮✮✮✮
High in Monounsaturated Fats	0
High in Polyunsaturated Fats	0
High in Iron	✮✮
Low in Sodium	✮✮✮✮✮✮✮
High in Potassium	✮✮✮✮
High in Calcium	✮✮✮✮
High in Vitamin A	✮✮✮✮✮✮✮
High in Vitamin C	✮✮✮✮✮✮✮
High in Vitamin B_6	✮✮✮✮✮✮
High in Folate	✮✮✮✮
Phytochemicals	✮✮✮✮✮✮✮

PAK CHOI

Scientific Name: *Brassica chinensis*
Other Common Names: Bok Choy (American English), Pok Choi, Chinese Cabbage, siu bok choy, pak choy

Origin and Background

The likely origin of Pak Choi is China and South East Asia. It was most likely introduced by the Chinese who came to the Caribbean to work on the plantations.

Varieties

There are two common varieties labelled pak choi– Chinese pak choi and Shanghai pak choi. They differ in appearance and texture. The Chinese pak choi is considered the traditional pak choi with dark leaves and crisp white stems. The Shanghai variety has lighter coloured leaves and green stems which are not as crisp as the Chinese pak choi.

Health and Dietary Benefits

Pak Choi aids healthy digestion due to the quality of dietary fibre. It contains powerful antioxidants and phytonutrients that help destroy free radicals around the body to protect cells and reduce inflammation. It is an excellent source of vitamin C which helps us to fight off infection and keep our immune systems robust. It is also a source of vitamin K to help keep our bones healthy and maintained. Pak Choi also provides calcium to add to bone protection and maintenance. Pak choi contains glucosinolates. These compounds have been reported to prevent cancer in small doses, but, like many substances, can be toxic to humans in large doses, particularly to people who are already seriously ill.

Preparation and Culinary Uses

The whole plant is edible, and it tastes cabbage-like with sweet undertones. It has a fabulously crisp texture. There are various ways of preparing this vegetable with both leaves and stalks imparting their own subtle flavours. Steamed, stir-fried, or added to soups or broths, it is still enjoyable. It can also be eaten raw in salads. It is recommended that this vegetable should be used within five days of purchase. Refrigerated storage is necessary.

Chinese pak choi is suitable for stir fries and for raw consumption. Shanghai pak choi can be used instead of the Chinese variety but should not be overcooked as it will become slimy.

RANK #5 – LETTUCE

Nutritional Criteria	Rating
High in Complex Carbohydrates	0
High in Dietary Fibre	☆☆
Low in Saturated Fats	★★★★★★★★★☆
High in Monounsaturated Fats	0
High in Polyunsaturated Fats	0
High in Iron	★★☆
Low in Sodium	★★★★★★★★★☆
High in Potassium	★★☆
High in Calcium	☆☆
High in Vitamin A	★★★★★★★☆
High in Vitamin C	★★★☆
High in Vitamin B$_6$	★★★☆
High in Folate	★★★★★☆
Phytochemicals	★★★★★★★☆

LETTUCE

Scientific Name: *Lactuca sativa*

Origin and Background

Lettuce was first cultivated in ancient Egypt to produce oil from its seeds. Evidence suggests cultivation since 2680 BC. The plant was later grown for its edible leaves.

Varieties

There are several varieties of lettuce. The main ones are Leaf lettuce which are red, green, and oak; Butterhead lettuce – with soft heads of thick oily-textured leaves; Romaine Lettuce: with its long, slightly bitter leaves and sturdy, sweeter centres and Iceberg lettuce, which is crisp and hearty, but not as flavourful as other lettuces. Iceberg is popular in the Caribbean.

Health and Dietary Benefits

Lettuce provides significant amounts of vitamins A and K. It is low in fibre but provides small amounts of many other healthy nutrients such as calcium, potassium, vitamin C, and folate. These nutrients can help to meet the standard daily requirements for body functions and can help to keep the immune system healthy.

Preparation and Culinary Uses

The art of preparing lettuce focuses on preserving the flavours, colour and crispness. When rinsing, the moisture should be inside the lettuce leaves not on top of them. Lettuce must then be drained properly. Droopy lettuce can often be rejuvenated in an iced water bath for about half an hour. Clean wet paper towel or a damp cloth also works well. The fridge dries out lettuce quickly. Delay this drying by covering with a clean damp cloth.

Lettuce is generally eaten raw, added to salads, sandwiches and wraps.

RANK # 6 – STRING BEANS

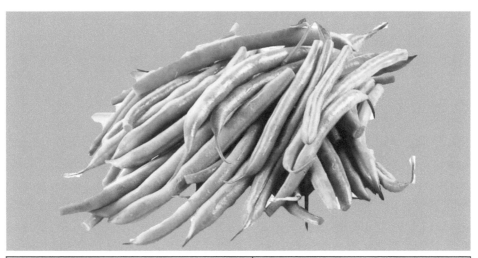

Nutritional Criteria	Rating
High in Complex Carbohydrates	★★
High in Dietary Fibre	★★★★
Low in Saturated Fats	★★★★★★★★★★
High in Monounsaturated Fats	0
High in Polyunsaturated Fats	0
High in Iron	★★
Low in Sodium	★★★★★★★★★★
High in Potassium	★★★★
High in Calcium	★★
High in Vitamin A	★★★★
High in Vitamin C	★★★★★★★★
High in Vitamin B$_6$	★★★★
High in Folate	★★★★
Phytochemicals	★★★★★★

STRING BEANS

Scientific Name: *Phaseolus vulgaris*
Other Common Names: Green beans, Snap Beans, Snaps, Haricots Vert

Origin and Background

String beans, also known as green beans, originated in Peru and spread to South and Central America by way of the migrating Indian tribes. It was most likely introduced into the Caribbean by Europeans and/or Chinese settlers.

Varieties

String beans are the unripe, young fruit and protective pods of various cultivars of the common bean (*Phaseolus vulgaris*. Over 130 varieties (cultivars) of string bean are known. Varieties specialized for use as green beans, selected for the succulence and flavour of their pods, are the ones usually grown in the home vegetable garden, and many varieties exist. Pod colour can be green, purple, red, or streaked. Shapes range from thin "fillet" types to wide "romano" types and more common types in between. Yellow-podded green beans are known as wax beans.

Health and Dietary Benefits

String beans contain many essential vitamins, including folate, a B vitamin that helps prevent neural tube defects and other birth defects. They are a good source of vitamin C, an antioxidant that helps boost the immune system. Vitamin C helps to produce collagen and protect the skin from oxidative stress. String beans also contain vitamin A which is important to immune health, reproduction, and healthy vision.

Preparation and Culinary Uses

String beans are sold fresh, canned, frozen, and dried. They are eaten around the world either raw, steamed, stir-fried, or baked in casseroles. Some US restaurants offer tempura-style green beans (seasoned, battered, and deep fried), or fried with vegetables such as carrots, corn, and peas, as vegetable chips. Green bean casserole is a popular dish throughout the USA, particularly at Thanksgiving. Fresh green beans are the healthiest option. Select beans that are bright green and free from black spots and blemishes. The beans should not be flimsy. For the optimal nutritional benefits, eat fresh green beans as soon as possible after harvesting or purchasing. Cooking green beans as well as thawing frozen green beans may cause a reduction in some nutrients such as vitamin C. Retain the nutrients by placing the frozen green beans in a small amount of water and cooking them for the least amount of time necessary. Fresh green beans should be refrigerated in a plastic bag and used within one week.

RANK #7 – CABBAGE

Nutritional Criteria	Rating
High in Complex Carbohydrates	0
High in Dietary Fibre	★ ★ ★ ★ ★ ☆
Low in Saturated Fats	★ ★ ★ ★ ★ ★ ★ ★ ★ ☆
High in Monounsaturated Fats	0
High in Polyunsaturated Fats	0
High in Iron	★ ★
Low in Sodium	★ ★ ★ ★ ★ ★ ★ ★ ★ ☆
High in Potassium	★ ★ ★
High in Calcium	★ ★
High in Vitamin A	★ ★
High in Vitamin C	★ ★ ★ ★ ★ ☆
High in Vitamin B$_6$	★ ★ ★ ★ ★ ☆
High in Folate	★ ★ ★ ☆
Phytochemicals	★ ★ ★ ★ ★ ☆

CABBAGE

Scientific Name: *Brassica oleracea*

Origin and Background

Cabbagenor headed cabbagemis a leafy green, red (purple), or white (pale green) biennial plant grown as an annual vegetable crop for its dense leaved heads. Cabbage was most likely domesticated somewhere in Europe before 1000 BC and was most likely introduced by the Europeans into the Caribbean.

Varieties

There are over 400 different varieties of cabbage grown throughout the world. Cultivars range from round to conical in shape with flat or curly, tight, or loose leaves which may be green, white, red, or purple in colour. Cabbage cultivars vary in their ability to store for extended periods of time. Dense-headed cultivars which mature slowly store for longer periods.

Health and Dietary Benefits

Cabbage is a rich source of vitamin C and vitamin K. It is also a moderate source of vitamin B_6 and folate. Cabbage is a good source of fibre and may therefore help lower the risk of certain diseases, improve digestion and combat inflammation. Cabbage is a source of indole-3-carbinol, a chemical under basic research for its possible properties. The evidence is unclear about whether compounds in cabbage such as phytochemicals may affect health or have anti-disease effects. Such compounds include sulforaphane and other glucosinolates which may stimulate the production of detoxifying enzymes during metabolism. Research on cruciferous vegetables such as cabbage, is on-going to determine if they have protective effects against colon cancer.

Preparation and Culinary Uses

Cabbage intended for long-term storage (5–6 months) should be stored at 0°C and 98–100% relative humidity. To store cabbage, wrap it tightly in plastic wrap if it has already been cut, or place in a sealable plastic bag if whole. The cabbage can then be stored in the crisper drawer of the refrigerator for up to 2 weeks.

Cabbage is prepared in many ways. It is consumed raw or steamed, though many cuisines stew, sautée and braise the cabbage. Pickling is one of the most popular ways of preserving cabbage, creating dishes such as sauerkraut and kimchi. The leaves can be blanched and used to wrap other ingredients to make stuffed cabbage.

Other Uses

Applying cabbage leaf compresses to the breast can result in relief of engorgement associated with improper breast feeding and could even contribute to reduced milk production and suppressed lactation. In this regard, extreme caution is recommended.

The popular 'cabbage soup diet' is intended to promote weight loss by severely restricting food intake. It is therefore not recommended as a healthy weight loss method.

RANK #8 – PUMPKIN

Nutritional Criteria	Rating
High in Complex Carbohydrates	☆☆
High in Dietary Fibre	☆☆☆☆
Low in Saturated Fats	☆☆☆☆☆☆☆☆☆☆
High in Monounsaturated Fats	0
High in Polyunsaturated Fats	0
High in Iron	☆☆
Low in Sodium	☆☆☆☆☆☆☆☆☆☆
High in Potassium	☆☆☆☆
High in Calcium	☆☆
High in Vitamin A	☆☆☆☆☆☆☆☆
High in Vitamin C	☆☆☆☆
High in Vitamin B$_6$	☆☆
High in Folate	0
Phytochemicals	☆☆☆☆☆☆☆☆☆

PUMPKIN

Scientific Name: *Cucurbita pepo*

Origin and Background

The word *pumpkin* originates from the word *pepon*, which is Greek for "large melon". The French adapted this word to *pompon*, which the British changed to *pumpion* and to the later American colonists, became known as *pumpkin*.

Pumpkins, like other squash, originated in northeastern Mexico and southern United States. The oldest evidence about pumpkin fragments dated between 7,000 and 5,500 BC found in Mexico.

Pumpkins are a warm-weather crop that is usually planted in early July. Pumpkins are, however, rather hardy, and even if many leaves and portions of the vine are removed or damaged, the plant can very quickly re-grow. Secondary vines replace what was removed.

Varieties

The term *pumpkin* is used interchangeably with "squash" and "winter squash". In North America and the United Kingdom, *pumpkin* traditionally refers to only certain round, orange varieties of winter squash, predominantly derived from *Cucurbita pepo*, while in Australian English, *pumpkin* can refer to winter squash of any appearance. In New Zealand and Australian English, the term *pumpkin* generally refers to the broader category called winter squash elsewhere.

Health and Dietary Benefits

Pumpkin is rich in vitamins, minerals and antioxidants which may boost your immune system, protect your eyesight, lower your risk of certain cancers and promote heart and skin health. Further its low calorie content makes it a weight-loss-friendly food. Pumpkin seeds, also known as *pepitas*, are edible and rich in nutrients. Pumpkin seeds are a good source of protein, magnesium, copper and zinc. Its fibre content aids with bowel function.

Preparation and Culinary Uses

When refrigerated they can last up to a week or so but can last much longer if frozen. Pumpkins are very versatile in their uses for cooking. Most parts of the pumpkin are edible, including the fleshy shell, the seeds, the leaves, and even the flowers. When ripe, the pumpkin can be steamed, roasted, or used as an ingredient in many dishes, especially soups. Pumpkin purée is sometimes prepared and frozen for later use. Within recent times, it has also found a place in the "Pongkin Crème" a substitute for Ponche de Creme, a Caribbean Christmas favourite, and in ketchup as a substitute for tomatoes. Pumpkin seeds are a popular snack that can be found hulled or semi-hulled at most grocery stores.

In its native North America, it is a very important traditional part of the autumn harvest, eaten mashed and making its way into soups and purees. Often, it is made into pie, various kinds of which are a traditional staple of the Canadian and American thanksgiving holidays. In the southwestern United States and Mexico, pumpkin and squash flowers are a popular and widely available food item. They may be used to garnish dishes, and they may be dredged in a batter then fried in oil. In Canada, Mexico, the United States, Europe and China, the seeds are often roasted and eaten as a snack. Pumpkins that are still small and green may be eaten in the same way as squash or zucchini.

Other Uses

Canned pumpkin is often recommended by veterinarians as a dietary supplement for dogs and cats that are experiencing certain digestive ailments such as constipation, diarrhea, or hairballs. Raw pumpkin can be fed to poultry, as a supplement to regular feed during the winter to help maintain egg production, which usually drops off during the cold months.

Pumpkins have been used as folk medicine by Native Americans to treat intestinal worms and urinary ailments, and this Native American remedy was adopted by American doctors in the early nineteenth century as an anthelmintic for the expulsion of worms. In Germany and south-eastern Europe, seeds of *C. pepo* were also used as folk remedies to treat irritable bladder and benign prostatic hyperplasia. In China, *C. moschata* seeds were also used in traditional Chinese medicine for the treatment of the parasitic disease schistosomiasis and for the expulsion of tape worms. Chinese studies have found that a combination of pumpkin seed and areca nut extracts was effective in the expulsion of *Taenia spp.* tapeworms in over 89% of cases. In the United States and Canada, pumpkin is a popular Halloween and Thanksgiving staple. They are commonly carved into decorative lanterns called jack-o'-lanterns for the Halloween season in North America.

RANK #9 – CARROT

Nutritional Criteria	Rating
High in Complex Carbohydrates	★★
High in Dietary Fibre	★★★★★★
Low in Saturated Fats	★★★★★★★★★★
High in Monounsaturated Fats	0
High in Polyunsaturated Fats	0
High in Iron	★★
Low in Sodium	★★★★★★★
High in Potassium	★★★
High in Calcium	0
High in Vitamin A	★★★★★★★★
High in Vitamin C	★★
High in Vitamin B$_6$	★★★★
High in Folate	0
Phytochemicals	★★★★★★★★

CARROT

Scientific Name: *Daucus carota*

Origin and Background

Carrots are a domesticated form of the wild carrot, native to Europe and southwestern Asia. The plant probably originated in Persia and was originally cultivated for its leaves and seeds. The most commonly eaten part of the plant is the taproot, although the stems and leaves can be eaten. The domestic carrot has been selectively bred for its greatly enlarged, more palatable, less woody-textured taproot. European settlers introduced the carrot to colonial America in the 17th century.

Varieties

There are many different varieties of carrots that can be found in various shapes, sizes and even colours. Carrots are most commonly orange in colour, but there are also carrots which are purple, yellow, red or white.

There are four main types of carrots, categorized based on shape. They are:

1. **Danvers** – most commonly known type. They are long, slender and tapered. They are usually orange coloured.
2. **Nantes** – rounded both at the tip and at the top. The flesh is a reddish colour and the flavour is noticeably sweet.
3. **Imperator** – similar in appearance to the Danvers but are thicker and wider.
4. **Chantenay** – short and broad.

Carrots may also be miniature.

Health and Dietary Benefits

Carrots consist of starch, fibre, and simple sugars. They are extremely low in fat and protein. Carrots are an excellent source of vitamin A in the form of beta carotene. They are also a good source of several B vitamins, vitamin K and potassium. Carrots are a good source of plant lutein which is related to vitamin A and beta carotene. Eating carrots is linked to a reduced risk of cancer and heart disease, as well as improved eye health. Additionally, this vegetable may be a valuable component of an effective weight loss diet.

Preparation and Culinary Uses

Carrots can be eaten in a variety of ways. They are probably the most universally palatable vegetable. Even children who dislike green vegetables are typically not averse to carrots. Sweet and crunchy when raw and even sweeter when cooked, carrots are definitely crowd pleasers. Carrots are versatile and can be eaten raw in salads, steamed, boiled and cooked in soups, stews and pies. Only 3 percent of the β-carotene in raw carrots is released during digestion. This can be improved to 39% by pulping, cooking and adding cooking oil. Alternatively, they may be chopped and fried or cooked and pureed into baby food.

The sweetness of carrots allows the vegetable to be used in some fruit-like roles. Grated carrots are used in carrot cakes, as well as carrot puddings. Carrots can also be used alone or blended with fruits in jams and preserves. Carrot juice is also widely marketed, especially as a health drink, either stand-alone or blended with juices extracted from fruits and other vegetables. Highly excessive consumption over a period of time results in a condition of carotenemia which is a yellowing of the skin caused by a build-up of carotenoids.

Carrots can be stored for several months in the refrigerator or over winter in a moist, cool place. For long term storage, unwashed carrots can be placed in a bucket between layers of sand, a 50/50 mix of sand and wood shavings, or in soil.

Other Uses

Carrots provide hair with vital vitamins, making your locks stronger, thicker and shinier. It could also brighten your skin. Carrots may also strengthen delicate tooth enamel.

RANK #10 – TOMATO

Nutritional Criteria	Rating
High in Complex Carbohydrates	0
High in Dietary Fibre	★★★
Low in Saturated Fats	★★★★★★★★★☆
High in Monounsaturated Fats	0
High in Polyunsaturated Fats	0
High in Iron	0
Low in Sodium	★★★★★★★★★☆
High in Potassium	★★
High in Calcium	0
High in Vitamin A	★★
High in Vitamin C	★★★★
High in Vitamin B$_6$	★★
High in Folate	★★★★
Phytochemicals	★★★★★★★★★☆

TOMATO

Scientific Name: *Solanum lycopersicum*
Other Common Names: Tomate, Love apple.

Origin and Background

Tomato was found among the early Aztecs around 700 A.D so it is native to South America, mainly in Peru, Bolivia, Chile, and Ecuador. It was not until around the 16th century that Europeans were introduced to it. In Europe it was grown as ornamental climbers and cultivated for its decorative leaves and fruit. Botanically tomato is a fruit, because it comes from a flower and contain seeds, but is generally eaten and prepared like a vegetable. It was originally thought to be poisonous because the plant belongs to the toxic nightshade family, but it requires a large and concentrated amount to induce sickness. It is now among the top four most popular vegetables eaten. Tomatoes are juicy and sweet, but they are often harvested while still green and immature, then ripened artificially with ethylene gas. This may lead to less flavor development, resulting in bland tomatoes.

Varieties

There are over 10,000 tomato cultivars. When they were first cultivated tomato varieties were yellow or orange. Through breeding, the standard colour of tomato varieties is now red. There are different types and sizes of tomato and the health benefits can vary between types. Tomatoes are usually red when mature but they can also come in a variety of colours, including yellow, orange, green, and purple. Many subspecies of tomatoes exist with different shapes and flavors.

Health and Dietary Benefits

Tomatoes are a good source of vitamin C, folate, and vitamin K. Fresh tomatoes are low in carbohydrates consisting mainly of simple sugars and insoluble fibres. Tomatoes contain key carotenoids such as lutein and copene which can protect the eye against light-induced damage. The antioxidant lycopene has been linked to many health benefits, including reduced risk of heart disease and cancer. The redder the tomato, the more lycopene it contains. Lycopene may help lower LDL cholesterol ("bad cholesterol"), reduce inflammation and markers of oxidative stress, and decrease the risk of blood clotting.

Preparation and Culinary Uses

Tomatoes are processed into products such as ketchup, tomato juice, tomato paste, and tomato sauces. Interestingly, the amount of lycopene in processed tomato products is often much higher than in fresh tomatoes. Processed tomatoes such as in ketchup are eaten in very small amounts. It is therefore better to acquire the lycopene by eating unprocessed tomatoes – which also have far less sugar than ketchup.

Other Uses

Tomato products are also known to be beneficial for skin health as it may protect against sunburns.

Vegetables

Nutritional Criteria	Callaloo	Dasheen Leaves	Spinach	Pak choi	Lettuce	String beans	Cabbage	Pumpkin	Carrot	Tomato
	1	2	3	4	5	6	7	8	9	10
High in Complex Carbohydrates	0	0	0	0	0	2	0	2	2	0
High in Dietary Fibre	8	8	8	4	2	4	6	4	6	3
Low in Saturated Fats	10	10	10	10	10	10	10	10	10	10
High in Monounsaturated Fats	0	0	0	0	0	0	0	0	0	0
High in Polyunsaturated Fats	0	0	0	0	0	0	0	0	0	0
High in Iron	8	8	8	2	3	2	2	2	2	0
Low in Sodium	6	10	8	8	10	10	10	10	8	10
High in Potassium	8	8	6	4	3	4	3	4	3	2
High in Calcium	8	8	4	4	2	2	2	2	0	0
High in Vitamin A	10	8	8	8	8	8	2	8	8	2
High in Vitamin C	8	8	8	8	4	8	6	4	2	4
High in Vitamin B$_6$	8	4	8	6	4	4	6	2	4	2
High in Folate	8	8	8	4	6	4	4	0	0	4
Phytochemicals	8	8	8	8	8	6	7	9	8	9

Summary of Ratings

BIBLIOGRAPHY

Bakhru, H.K. (1995). *Foods That Heal: The Natural Way to Good Health*. Retrieved from https://books.google.com.jm/books/about/Foods_That_Heal.html?id=jy-qzV-tcDRQC&redir_esc=y

Balliu, Astrit. (2014). Cabbage. Retrieved from https://www.researchgate.net/publication/280943039_Cabbage

Callaloo Wikipedia Page https://en.wikipedia.org/wiki/Callaloo

CTA. (2016). Callaloo. Retrieved from http://chefs4dev.org/index.php/local-products/callaloo/index.html

Dias, J. (2014). Nutritional and Health Benefits of Carrots and Their Seed Extracts. *Food and Nutrition Sciences*. 05. 2147-2156. 10.4236/fns.2014.522227.

Healthaholics. (2017). Benefits of Spinach. Retrieved from https://tgraph.io/BENE-FITS-OF-SPINACH-03-07

Higman, B.W. (2007). *Callaloo*. Johns Hopkins University Press Volume 30, Number 1, Winter. 351-368 10.1353/cal.2007.0137

Karthikeyan, M., Gnanasekaran, A., Rashmi., Ts, Gopenath.,Palanisamy, P. & Gk, Chandrashekrappa & Basalingappa, Kanthesh & Bm, Kanthesh. (2018). *Taro (Colocasia esculenta): An overview*. 156–161.

Lim, A., Ji-Ah, S., Hur, M.,Lee, Mi-Kyoung & Lee, M.S. (2016). Cabbage compression early breast care on breast engorgement in primiparous women after cesarean birth: A controlled clinical trial. *International Journal of Clinical and Experimental Medicine*. 8. 21335–42.

McDermott, A. (2017). Green Beans: Nutrition Facts and Health Benefits. Retrieved from https://www.healthline.com/health/food-nutrition/green-beans#vitamins-and-minerals-folate

Price, R. & Price, S. (1992). Callaloo. New West Indian Guide / Nieuwe West-Indische Gids. 66. 10.1163/13822373-90002008.

Roughani, A.,& Miri, S. M. (2019). *Spinach: An important green leafy vegetable and medicinal herb*.

Sharma, R. (2018). Effectiveness of Chilled Cabbage Leaf Application on Breast Engorgement among Post Partum Women's. *Journal of Medical Science And clinical Research*. 6. 10.18535/jmscr/v6i6.147.

Simon, P., Freeman, R., Vieira, J., & Boiteux, L., & Briard, M., & Nothnagel, T., Michalik, B., & Kwon, Y. (2008). Carrot. 10.1007/978-0-387-74110-9_8.

Wikipedia. Carrot. Retrieved from https://en.wikipedia.org/wiki/Carrot

Wikipedia. Spinach. Retrieved from https://en.wikipedia.org/wiki/Spinach

Wikipedia. Pumpkin. Retrieved from https://en.wikipedia.org/wiki/Pumpkin

Wikipedia. Green Bean. Retrieved from https://en.wikipedia.org/wiki/Green_bean https://en.wikipedia.org/wiki/Colocasia_esculenta

4 LEGUMES, NUTS AND SEEDS

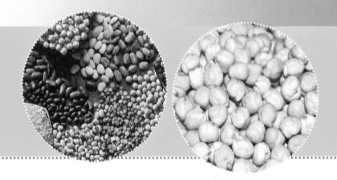

Legumes are classified as beans (*Phaseolus)*, peas/edible seeds and lentils (*Lens)*. This food group may also include nuts and seeds. Legumes can be found across the globe and have been in cultivation for thousands of years in both tropical and temperate climates. Legumes were among the first crops cultivated. Beans were discovered in the tombs of the Pharaohs and Aztecs. The ancient Egyptians considered beans to be a symbol of life and had temples dedicated to them. Later, the Greeks and Romans used them in festivals to worship their gods. The four most distinguished Roman families were named after beans: *Fabius* (fava bean), *Lentulus* (lentil), *Piso* (pea), and *Cicero* (chickpea).

Only cereals have a higher rank than legumes in providing calories and protein for the world's population. Legumes provide about the same number of calories per unit of weight as cereals but about 2 to 4 times more protein. Legumes are the best source of concentrated protein in the plant kingdom and are close to animal meat in quality. Being of plant origin, legumes are cholesterol-free. Their soluble fibre content helps in reducing serum cholesterol thus lowering the risk of heart disease. Legumes contain phytochemicals (isoflavones) which have been associated with reduced risks of several chronic diseases. Legumes combined with grains complement the amino acids that are deficient in grains thus providing complete protein.

Lectins are proteins found in almost all foods, especially legumes. It is claimed that lectins cause increased gut permeability and drive autoimmune diseases. Although certain lectins are toxic and cause harm when consumed in excess, they are easy to get rid of through cooking. It is recommended that beans should be soaked before cooking. The water should be changed periodically as this helps to reduce the indigestible complex sugars that create gas in the intestines. Some of the indigestible complex sugars are absorbed in the water.

Nuts come in various shapes and sizes. Nuts are available in the Caribbean in all seasons and thus used frequently. Most nuts come from the seeds or dried fruits of trees and have an outer shell that both protects the nut and keeps the healthy fats inside the nut from spoiling. Nuts contain up to 85% unsaturated fats. This amount is similar to what is found in avocados and olive oil. These good, monounsaturated fats have been known to help lower cholesterol levels and also reduce the risk of heart disease.

Nuts are a good source of B vitamins, particularly thiamine, riboflavin, and niacin. These nutrients help to boost energy production and promote healthy cell reproduction. However, the process of roasting nuts will inherently destroy most nutrients, especially thiamine, while raw and sprouted nuts retain thiamine. Nuts are also valuable sources of vitamin E, and in addition to helping the body to effectively use some nutrients, they may help protect against the damaging effects of free radicals. Nuts also provide some vitamin K which is important to help with clotting of blood and prevent excessive bleeding following an injury. Although friendly bacteria in the intestines produce much of the vitamin K that is needed by the body, about 20% of it should be obtained from food such as nuts.

Seeds are usually small in size but are nutrient-dense. They provide the hard-to-get nutrients such as plant protein, zinc, iron, copper, selenium, calcium, magnesium, vitamin E, and B vitamins. Seeds are highly recommended as part of a healthy diet because they help to lower cholesterol, stabilize blood sugar, reduce risk for colon cancer and improve bowel health. Each variety of seed contains a unique mix of nutrients and phytochemicals to promote health and fight disease.

RANK #1 – CHICKPEAS

Nutritional Criteria	Rating
High in Complex Carbohydrates	★ ★ ★ ★ ★ ★ ★ ☆
High in Dietary Fibre	★ ★ ★ ★ ★ ★ ★ ★ ★ ☆
Low in Saturated Fats	★ ★ ★ ★ ★ ★ ★ ★ ☆
High in Monounsaturated Fats	★ ☆
High in Polyunsaturated Fats	★ ★ ★ ☆
High in Iron	★ ★ ★ ★ ★ ★ ☆
Low in Sodium	★ ★ ★ ★ ★ ★ ★ ★ ☆
High in Potassium	★ ★ ★ ★ ★ ★ ☆
High in Calcium	★ ☆
High in Vitamin A	0
High in Vitamin C	★ ★ ★ ☆
High in Vitamin B$_6$	★ ★ ★ ★ ★ ★ ★ ★ ★ ☆
High in Folate	★ ★ ★ ★ ★ ★ ★ ★ ☆
Phytochemicals	★ ★ ★ ★ ★ ★ ☆

CHICKPEAS

Scientific Name: *Cicer arietinum*
Other Common Names: Channa, Garbanzo Beans

Origin and Background

Chickpeas or Channa is the most widely consumed high-protein legume in the world. It originated in the Middle East and it is believed that the legume became known as a chickpea after the French word "pois chiche." As it became widespread in England, chickpeas became known as "chiche pease." Another name for this item is *"Garbanzo Bean"* which comes from the Spanish term for chickpea, a compound of "garau" meaning "seed," and "antzu" meaning "dry."

Varieties

Chickpeas are grown worldwide. The two main varieties are Kabuli and Desi. **Kabuli** type is also known as Garbanzo bean and is grown mainly in the Mediterranean region, South America, and in Southeast Asia. These are increasingly common in American groceries and the Caribbean. They are large and beige in colour with a thin skin, and have a mild nutty, creamy flavour. **Green chickpeas** are young garbanzo beans that are harvested early while in its immature, green state thus the green colour and sweet flavour, almost like green peas. **The Desi** type is more popular worldwide and is also called **Black chickpeas (Bengal gram or Kala channa)** and is grown mainly in India, East Africa, Mexico, and Iran. They are small with a light to deep rust/brown colour, a yellow interior and a thick, rough skin (seed coat). They have an earthy aroma and a nutty flavour. The seed coat is more nutritious than the Kabuli-type. The dark seed coat can be removed, and the seed split in half to make *'Chana Dahl'*, *Chana Dal*, or *Bengal gram*, also known as *split desi-chickpea* or *yellow gram*. Chickpeas are available either dried or canned.

Health and Dietary Benefits

Chickpeas are nutrient dense. They are high in protein, vitamins B_6 and folate; rich in the minerals: potassium and iron and a good source of complex carbohydrates. Additionally, it is low in the mineral sodium, high in dietary fibre and rich in phytochemicals. These characteristics are responsible for most of their health benefits, which range from weight management to improving blood sugar levels due to a low glycaemic index, especially applicable to the Desi variety. The high protein and fibre content make them a filling food that may help control appetite and reduce calorie intake of meals. The high fibre content also benefits digestion by increasing the number of healthy bacteria in your gut and helping waste flow efficiently through your digestive tract. Regular consumption may reduce your risk of developing chronic diseases, such as heart disease and cancer. Chickpeas are an excellent meat alternative for vegetarians and vegans due to their protein content.

Preparation and Culinary Uses

Dried chickpeas must be cooked for some time until the desired tenderness is reached but cooking time can be reduced by pressurizing or soaking a few hours in advance. The longer they are stored, the more moisture they will lose and the longer they will take to cook. Chickpeas are also available canned, a form which retains the shape and flavour of chickpeas well. However, before using, rinsing and draining are necessary to get rid of most of the added sodium and any canned taste before using. Green Chickpeas do not need to be reconstituted with water. They are harvested from the field, washed, blanched and flash frozen, locking in the natural colour, moisture, nutrition and flavour.

Chickpeas can be eaten as a "side dish" either boiled or curried, used cold in salads, added to soups and stews, ground and shaped into balls and fried as *falafel* or cooked with rice, pasta or other foods. It can also be an item that can be included in complementary feeds for infants. Chickpeas are a delicious snack for almost all age groups when fried dry and seasoned. Chickpeas can also be made into a dish called *hummus,* a paste mixed with tahini (sesame seed paste). In the Caribbean, and among persons from this Region, chickpeas are a primary and favourite ingredient in roti and doubles.

Other Uses

The livestock industry is provided with an alternative protein and energy feedstuff.

RANK #2 – RED BEANS

Nutritional Criteria	Rating
High in Complex Carbohydrates	★★★★★☆
High in Dietary Fibre	★★★★★★★★★☆
Low in Saturated Fats	★★★★★★★★★☆
High in Monounsaturated Fats	0
High in Polyunsaturated Fats	0
High in Iron	★★★★★★★☆
Low in Sodium	★★★★★★★★★☆
High in Potassium	★★★★★★★☆
High in Calcium	★★★★
High in Vitamin A	0
High in Vitamin C	★★
High in Vitamin B$_6$	★★★★★★★☆
High in Folate	★★★★★★★★★☆
Phytochemicals	★★★★★★★☆

RED BEANS

Scientific Name *Phaseolus vulgaris*
Other Common Names: Kidney beans, Rajma, Mexican Beans

Origin and Background

The red bean is a kidney-shaped bean with a subtle sweet flavour and soft texture that generally keep its shape during cooking. It is available either dried or canned. Red kidney beans are thought to have originated in Peru and are native to Central America and Mexico. It has been a common inclusion in the diet of the Indians of the Americas. Planted by Spanish settlers, kidney beans were cultivated in Louisiana in the late 1700s. It is recorded that during this period, Haitians emigrated to New Orleans bringing spicy Caribbean recipes for beans and rice.

Varieties

The most common variety is red in colour. Other common varieties are dark red, spotted, striped, and mottled.

Health and Dietary Benefits

Kidney beans are an excellent plant-based source of protein and an excellent meat substitute. Kidney beans also provide a variety of minerals: being rich in potassium, a good source of iron, a fair source of calcium and the dried form is low in sodium. Additionally, they provide a small amount of vitamin C – a strong antioxidant, high in folate and are a good source of vitamin B_6 and phytochemicals, which are unique plant compounds. They are useful to control appetite as a part of a weight reducing diet, while also promoting colon health and moderating blood sugar levels due to their dietary fibre content.

Preparation and Culinary Uses

Dried kidney beans should be soaked before cooking and cooked well because they contain toxins on the outer skin when raw. These toxins are rendered harmless by boiling. Canned beans should be drained before use. Red beans are a favourite in Caribbean cuisine, with Jamaica being noted for a dish called rice and peas. Kidney beans can be used in various ways such as a "side dish", in soups, salads or stews. A traditional dish in Latin America is Refried beans.

RANK #3 – LIMA BEANS

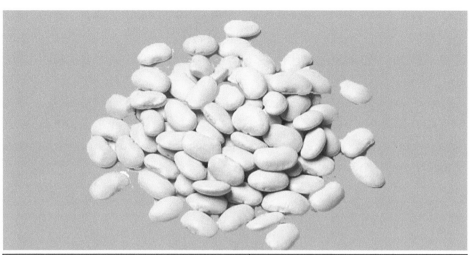

Nutritional Criteria	Rating
High in Complex Carbohydrates	★★★★★☆
High in Dietary Fibre	★★★★★★★★★☆
Low in Saturated Fats	★★★★★★★★★☆
High in Monounsaturated Fats	0
High in Polyunsaturated Fats	0
High in Iron	★★★★★★★☆
Low in Sodium	★★★★★★★★☆
High in Potassium	★★★★★★★★★☆
High in Calcium	★★★☆
High in Vitamin A	0
High in Vitamin C	0
High in Vitamin B_6	★★★★★★★★★☆
High in Folate	★★★★★★★★★☆
Phytochemicals	★★★★★☆

LIMA BEANS

Scientific Name: *Phaseolus Lunatus*
Other Common Names: Lima peas, Madagascar Bean

Origin and Background

The Lima bean is a tropical and sub-tropical legume grown for its edible seeds, not the pods. It is reported to have originated in Peru. The bean carries the same name as the capital of Peru (Lima), and it is entrenched in Peruvian culture appearing as a symbol of war and eternal life on art and pottery of the Moche people who inhabited northern Peru in the 15th century. Native American Indians also cultivated this crop in the southern part of the United States, and it was brought to Europe in the 16th century by explorers. Today the beans are popular worldwide but are used to a lesser extent in the Caribbean.

Varieties

Botanically, there are two varieties, namely *Silvester,* the wild variety, and the domesticated variety, *Lunatus.* Another description is the large-seeded/pole and small-seeded/bush varieties. The large variety are moon-shaped, are commonly called butter beans and are often sold as dried beans. These have a buttery flavour and starchy texture. The small-seeded variety are pale green and are commonly known as baby limas. These are milder and less starchy than large lima beans, which have an earthy flavour.

Health and Dietary Benefits

Lima beans provide a variety of minerals: excellent source of potassium and molybdenum; a good source of copper, manganese, phosphorus; magnesium, and iron, and a fair amount of calcium. Additionally, they are an excellent source of dietary fibre, vitamins B_6 and folate and provide high-quality protein. Lima beans also contain phytochemicals and are a natural detoxifying food.

Preparation and Culinary Uses

Raw lima beans contain linamarin, which when consumed, decomposes into the toxic chemical hydrogen cyanide. The edible seeds should be cooked for at least 10 minutes to render them safe. Soaking the lima beans in water for at least 8 hours is recommended to help remove some of the sugars, thus making the beans easier to digest. It is a key ingredient in succotash (North America) and paella, a rice dish that originated in Spain. The beans can be boiled, fried, ground into powder and baked, and used in soups and stews.

Other Uses

After harvesting, the vines, leaves and empty pods can be used as fodder, made into hay or silage. Lima beans may be used as green manure or a cover crop and may also be useful for intercropping systems.

RANK #4 – LENTILS

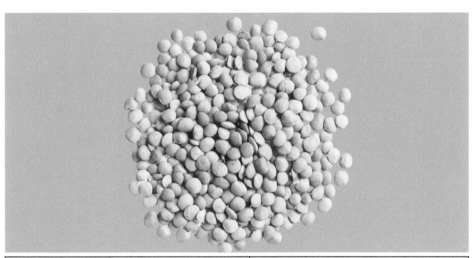

Nutritional Criteria	Rating
High in Complex Carbohydrates	★★★★
High in Dietary Fibre	★★★★★★★★
Low in Saturated Fats	★★★★★★★★★
High in Monounsaturated Fats	0
High in Polyunsaturated Fats	0
High in Iron	★★★★★★★
Low in Sodium	★★★★★★★★★
High in Potassium	★★★★★★
High in Calcium	★★
High in Vitamin A	0
High in Vitamin C	★★
High in Vitamin B$_6$	★★★★★★★★★
High in Folate	★★★★★★★
Phytochemicals	★★★★★

LENTILS

Scientific Name: *Lens Culinaris*
Other Common Names: Green, French, Spanish Brown, Dhal Lentils, Black Beluga Lentils

Origin and Background

Lentils are small legume seeds that are believed to have originated in the Near East or Mediterranean area and are the oldest known domesticated pulse crop. Lentils are grown throughout the world, are relatively tolerant to drought but grow best in cool weather. The Lentil is shaped like the double convex optic lens thus its name *lentil* from the Latin *lens*. Lentils were considered a delicacy for the upper class, but is also called a poor man's food because it was popular among this sector who could not afford fish during Lent. Thus, they were used as a substitute for fish. On Good Friday, it is still a popular choice in some Caribbean countries. Lentils have an earthy, nutty flavor and are prominent in the cuisine of many nations.

Varieties

There are many types of lentils. The four most popular are: Brown lentils, the cheapest and soften the most during cooking; Green lentils that have a nuttier flavor and stay firm when cooked; Red lentils that have a milder taste and Black lentils, also known as beluga lentils, as they look like caviar when cooked. In cuisines of the Indian subcontinent, split lentils are known as dal. Pale brown lentils are the most common variety used in the Caribbean.

Health and Dietary Benefits

Lentils add essential vitamins and minerals to the diet. They are rich in protein, iron, vitamin B_6, folate and dietary fibre; a good source of potassium, and phytochemicals but are low in fat. The folic acid and potassium all support heart health, and the fibre helps to promote blood sugar control.

Preparation and Culinary Uses

Very versatile, lentils are best if cooked with assertive flavorings or other foods in combination with robust, zesty sauces. Unlike other dried beans and peas, lentils are easy to cook, quick-cooking and there's no need for soaking before cooking. However, they should be searched for the presence of small stones, pieces of woody stems and/or other inedible particles.

Generally, lentils maintain their shape during and after cooking. This versatile bean can be prepared alone as a side dish, converted into paté, loaf, balls; used in soups, added to rice, and used in many other ways. Brown lentils are best used in soups and stews; Green lentils are good for salad or taco toppers and Red lentils are used for Indian dals and purees.

RANK # 5 – PIGEON PEAS

Nutritional Criteria	Rating
High in Complex Carbohydrates	★★★★★☆
High in Dietary Fibre	★★★★★★★★★☆
Low in Saturated Fats	★★★★★★★★★☆
High in Monounsaturated Fats	0
High in Polyunsaturated Fats	0
High in Iron	★★★★★★★☆
Low in Sodium	★★★★★★★★★☆
High in Potassium	★★★★★★★☆
High in Calcium	★★★☆
High in Vitamin A	0
High in Vitamin C	0
High in Vitamin B_6	★★★★★★★☆
High in Folate	★★★★★★★☆
Phytochemicals	★★★★★★★☆

PIGEON PEAS, DRIED AND GREEN

Scientific Name: *Cajanus Cajan*
Other Common Names: Gungo

Origin and Background

The pigeon pea was domesticated in the Indian subcontinent over 3,500 years ago. Now its seeds have become a common food in Asia, Africa, Latin America, and the Caribbean where it is popular in the cuisine. This short lifespan shrub is also known as the tropical green pea. Their shape is either round, globular or oval. Pigeon peas develop in small to medium sized pea pods, with an average of four to five developed seeds per pod.

Varieties

The peas come in a variety of colours ranging from bright green when young to a goldenrod yellow or brownish to almost purple or black when mature, and could include streaks of purple, or black. The green variety is sometimes available frozen. In the dried form, they are brown and are available all year round either packaged or canned.

Health and Dietary Benefits

To date, several flavonoids, isoflavonoids, tannins and protein fractions have been isolated from its different parts and their medicinal uses have been established. It has anti-inflammatory properties. One of the key minerals found in pigeon peas is potassium, known to regulate blood pressure and improve heart health. Other nutrients that pigeon peas contribute in significant amounts include iron, vitamin B_6 and folate. Pigeon peas may support growth and development, prevent anaemia, boost energy and strengthen the immune system.

Preparation and Culinary Uses

Fresh pigeon peas are nutty in taste and offer a crispy texture. A versatile food that can be cooked like other legumes or curried. Trinidad and Tobago, and Grenada have their own national dish, called *pelau*, which includes either beef or chicken, and occasionally pumpkin or carrots and maybe pieces of cured pig tail or beef.

Other Uses

Pigeon peas are grown primarily as a grain crop seed for human consumption, but it has many other uses. The foliage may be cut and fed to livestock fresh or conserved. Stems are used for firewood. It is sometimes used as a semi-permanent, perennial component in alley cropping systems. They are grown as hedgerow for windbreaks, and as ground cover or shade cover for establishing plantation crops, e.g. coffee. It has good nitrogen fixation properties which makes it a useful green manure.

RANK #6 – COW PEAS

Nutritional Criteria	Rating
High in Complex Carbohydrates	★★★★
High in Dietary Fibre	★★★★★★★★
Low in Saturated Fats	★★★★★★★★★★
High in Monounsaturated Fats	0
High in Polyunsaturated Fats	0
High in Iron	★★★★★★★★★★
Low in Sodium	★★★★★★★★★★
High in Potassium	★★★★★★★★★★
High in Calcium	★★★★
High in Vitamin A	0
High in Vitamin C	0
High in Vitamin B$_6$	★★★★★★★★
High in Folate	★★★★★★★★★★
Phytochemicals	★★★★★★

COW PEAS

Scientific Name: *Vigna Unguiculata*
Other Common Names: Black eye peas

Origin and Background

Cowpeas were cultivated to feed cows, thus its name. Cowpeas came to the Caribbean via ships that carried distressed slaves. They are often considered as poor man's food due to its humble origins. The uses of cowpeas date back to Jamaica around 1675. The cowpea plant can thrive in many conditions and can grow in various weather conditions. They are a staple in Indian cuisine and are also used to create stews in South Africa. South America boasts one of the largest cultivations of cowpeas and it is an important addition to their daily diets.

Varieties

Several cultivars of cowpeas are grown and categorized based on their seed type and colour: Black-eyed and purple-eyed beans are kidney shaped with blunt ends. Their skin is cream-white with white hilum surrounded by black, pink, or light-red stain. The peas shell easily, and shelled peas are attractive, mild flavored and suitable for processing. Brown eyed peas feature white hilum surrounded by brown skin. The pods vary in colour from green to purple and have a wide range of lengths. Crowder-Seeds in the pods are closely crowded and tend to be globular in shape. Cream beans-The cream-coloured seeds of the cream beans feature inconspicuous hilum (no noticeable "eye").

Health and Dietary Benefits

Cowpeas health benefits include improving digestion, supporting heart health, detoxifying the body, treating insomnia, managing diabetes, and supporting blood circulation. Other health benefits include preventing anaemia, supporting weight loss, supporting healthy skin, fighting free radicals, and maintaining healthier bones. They are a rich source of fibre and have been known to ease stomach conditions such as diarrhoea and constipation. Bulking up the stool promotes adequate passage of faeces through the intestinal tract and relieves the digestive system of unfavourable conditions. The dietary fibre also helps keep the overall digestive system in check. Cowpeas are abundant and their nutritional value is far higher than most fancy foods. They can provide a good amount of minerals and vitamins to the body. They can be added to stews, curries and salads to increase protein and carbohydrates. All varieties of cowpeas are very good sources of vegetarian protein.

Preparation and Culinary Uses

The raw, green pods of black-eyed pea are edible before they fully mature and are often served as a green vegetable. Although soaking is not mandatory for cowpeas, it quickens overall cooking time, removes anti-nutritional compounds, and enriches flavor Whole beans may take about one hour to cook. Pressure-cook for 10 minutes after soaking or 10–20 minutes without soaking. Avoid overcooking which can result in a pureed product. Almost all parts of this plant are edible and contain vast nutrients. Black-eyed peas can be used in soups and salads, shaped into patties, loaf or balls or slow cooked. They are made into puree or sprouted.

Other Uses

Cowpeas provide a large amount of nitrogen to the soil in which they grow. They act as a soil fixer for other plants and are often considered green manure. Consuming black-eyed peas on Old Year's Night/New Year's Eve has become a tradition and is associated with prosperity during the upcoming year.

RANK # 7 – BROAD BEANS

Nutritional Criteria	Rating
High in Complex Carbohydrates	★★★☆
High in Dietary Fibre	★★★★★★★★★☆
Low in Saturated Fats	★★★★★★★★★☆
High in Monounsaturated Fats	0
High in Polyunsaturated Fats	0
High in Iron	★★★★★★☆
Low in Sodium	★★★★★★★★★☆
High in Potassium	★★★★★★☆
High in Calcium	★★★★
High in Vitamin A	0
High in Vitamin C	★★★★
High in Vitamin B$_6$	★★★★★★★☆
High in Folate	★★★★★★☆
Phytochemicals	★★★★★☆

BROAD BEANS

Scientific Name: *Vicia Faba*

Other Common Names: Fava, Butterbean, Windsor Bean, English Bean

133

Origin and Background

The broad bean is a temperate crop which originated in the Mediterranean region or southwestern Asia.

Varieties

There exist many varieties of broad bean, classified in three groups according to the size of the pod: long pod, Windsor, and dwarf pod.

Health and Dietary Benefits

Broad beans contain starch and low amounts of sugar, fat, and sodium. Their fibre content helps to protect against intestinal cancer and diabetes. They are also a good source of polyphenolic compounds, with an antioxidant activity that may provide protection against coronary diseases and cancer. Broad beans are rich in proteins and provide modest amounts of iron and vitamin B, like thiamine and riboflavin. Thiamine is essential for good health – a deficiency of which causes beriberi. Broad beans must not be eaten raw. They must be cooked in order to denature the toxic haemagglutinins. They are also good sources of potassium, vitamin E, beta-carotene and quercetin flavonoid and a fair amount of vitamin C.

Broad beans are an excellent vegetable source of protein and fibre. This may be a winning combination for weight loss. Broad beans are also rich in both folate and B vitamins, which are needed for nerve and blood cell development, cognitive function, and energy.

Preparation and Culinary Uses

The seeds and pods can be cooked in many ways, such as boiled and pureed, or even consumed as a summer soup. Their superior leaves can even be used as spinach.

Preparing broad beans involves first removing the beans from their pods, followed by soaking and steaming or parboiling to loosen and remove their tough exterior coat or outer skin. Broad beans have a creamy texture; with a nutty, sweet earthy flavour. They can be used in soups, or puréed into paté like hummus with rosemary, olive oil, garlic, lemon, and fresh herbs added.

They are a good accompaniment to blanched cauliflower pieces, with olive oil, chopped red onion, and balsamic vinegar. Use caution when pressure cooking because of the loose skins.

RANK #8 – PEANUTS

Nutritional Criteria	Rating
High in Complex Carbohydrates	★★
High in Dietary Fibre	★★★★★★★☆
Low in Saturated Fats	★★★★★☆
High in Monounsaturated Fats	★★★★★★★☆
High in Polyunsaturated Fats	★★★★
High in Iron	★★★★★☆
Low in Sodium	★★★★★★★★★☆
High in Potassium	★★★★★★★☆
High in Calcium	★★★★
High in Vitamin A	0
High in Vitamin C	0
High in Vitamin B$_6$	★★★★
High in Folate	★★★★
Phytochemicals	★★★★

PEANUTS

Scientific Name: *Arachis hypogea*
Other Common Names: Groundnuts, Earth Nuts, Goobers.

Origin and Background

Peanuts originated in South America. They grow on small bushes unlike most other nuts which grow on trees. Technically, they are not nuts. They are considered part of the legume family.

Varieties

There are four basic varieties of peanuts: Runner, Virginia, Spanish and Valencia. Each of the peanut types is distinctive in size, flavour, and nutritional composition.

Health and Dietary Benefits

Peanuts are highly nutritious seeds. They are popular and have been associated with many health benefits. Compared with other nuts, they have a good balance of amino acids providing about 25% to 30% protein; many minerals such as iron, magnesium, phosphorus, zinc and copper; more B-vitamins, except B_{12}. Although they are relatively high in fat, most of it is monounsaturated, the healthier type of fat. Peanuts are a good source of omega-3 fatty acids, fibre, vitamin E, and antioxidants. They can be useful as a part of a weight loss diet and may reduce the risk of both heart disease and gallstones.

Preparation and Culinary Uses

Peanuts can be added to salads, stir-fried dishes or can be processed into commercial or home-made peanut butter. Peanuts are available shelled or unshelled and are often roasted and salted. They are ideal for snacking but should be consumed in moderation because of the fat content. Because peanuts are high in fat, they need to be stored in a cool, dry place in an airtight container, or refrigerated to prevent rancidity. A common by-product is peanut oil which can be used in cooking or added to many commercial products. Other products made from peanuts include peanut flour, and peanut protein. Peanut products are used in a variety of foods, desserts, cakes, confectionery, snacks, and sauces.

RANK #9 – PUMPKIN SEEDS

Nutritional Criteria	Rating
High in Complex Carbohydrates	0
High in Dietary Fibre	★★★★★☆
Low in Saturated Fats	★★★☆
High in Monounsaturated Fats	★★★★★☆
High in Polyunsaturated Fats	★★★★★☆
High in Iron	★★★★★☆
Low in Sodium	★★★★★★★★★☆
High in Potassium	★★★★★★★☆
High in Calcium	★★
High in Vitamin A	0
High in Vitamin C	0
High in Vitamin B$_6$	★★★☆
High in Folate	★★★☆
Phytochemicals	★★★★★☆

PUMPKIN SEEDS

Scientific Names: *Cucurbita pepo, Cucurbita maxima, Cucurbita moschata, Cucurbita mixta.*

Other Common Names: Pepitas, Spanish for "little seed of squash."

Origin and Background

Pumpkin seeds are flat, dark green seeds. They are native to the Americas, and indigenous species are found across North America, South America, and Central America. The seeds have a high-fat content, so they are prone to rancidity. Keep pumpkin seeds in a cool, dark, and dry place to improve shelf life. If stored properly, pumpkin seeds will keep for 3–4 months.

Varieties

Some pumpkin seeds are encased in a yellow-white husk (often called the "shell"), although some varieties of pumpkins produce seeds without shells. Pumpkin seeds have a malleable, chewy texture and a subtly sweet, nutty flavour. While roasted pumpkins seeds are probably best known for their role as a perennial Halloween treat, these seeds are so delicious, and nutritious, that they can be enjoyed throughout the year. In many food markets, pepitas are available in all the forms described above – raw and shelled, raw and unshelled, roasted and shelled or roasted and unshelled.

Health and Dietary Benefits

Pumpkin seeds are rich sources of many minerals including manganese, magnesium, phosphorus, and zinc. These minerals may help protect bones from osteoporotic fractures. There is increasing evidence that pumpkin seeds also promote prostate health because they contain a phytochemical called cucurbitacin, which reduces the risk of prostate cancer. The fatty acids in pumpkin seeds contain other beneficial nutrients, such as sterols, squalene, and tocopherols. Pumpkin seeds also contain omega-3 and omega-6 fatty acids, antioxidants, and fibre. This combination has benefits for both the heart and liver. The fibre in pumpkin seeds helps lower the total amount of cholesterol in the blood and decrease the risk of heart disease.

Without the side effects of the drug, pumpkin seeds compare favorably to the anti-inflammatory drug indomethacin in reducing inflammatory symptoms.

Preparation and Culinary Uses

Pumpkin seeds can easily be added to sautéed vegetables, salads, dressings, cereals, burgers, and more. Pumpkin seeds can also be scooped from the pumpkin roasted and used as a snack.

RANK #10 – GREEN SPLIT PEAS

Nutritional Criteria	Rating
High in Complex Carbohydrates	★ ★ ☆
High in Dietary Fibre	★ ★ ★ ★ ★ ★ ★ ★ ☆
Low in Saturated Fats	★ ★ ★ ★ ★ ★ ★ ★ ☆
High in Monounsaturated Fats	0
High in Polyunsaturated Fats	0
High in Iron	★ ☆
Low in Sodium	★ ★ ★ ★ ★ ★ ★ ★ ☆
High in Potassium	★ ★ ★ ★ ★ ★ ☆
High in Calcium	0
High in Vitamin A	0
High in Vitamin C	☆
High in Vitamin B$_6$	★ ★ ★ ★ ★ ☆
High in Folate	★ ★ ★ ☆
Phytochemicals	★ ★ ★ ☆

GREEN SPLIT PEAS

Scientific Names: *Pisum Sativum*

Origin and Background

Split peas have a long history and have been used in many cuisines as early as 400–500 BC in Athens where they were sold by street vendors. The ancient Greeks, Romans, and Egyptians all cultivated and consumed these peas.

Varieties

There are green and yellow varieties of split peas. Yellow peas are milder than the green variety. Both have a grainy texture and do not hold their shape during cooking. Green split peas are sweeter and less starchy than the milder yellow split peas which are more frequently used in the Caribbean in a variety of ways, particularly among ethnic East Indians.

Health and Dietary Benefits

Split peas offer significant levels of protein, zinc, and phosphorus and a small amount of iron. A diet rich in split peas and other legumes may help reduce cholesterol, hypertension, and the risk of prediabetes, and may also offer significant anti-inflammatory effects. Split peas contain high amounts of dietary fibre.

Preparation and Culinary Uses

Soaking peas overnight in water shortens their cooking time, but this process is not entirely necessary. Split peas cook relatively quickly.

In the Caribbean split peas are a key ingredient in many East Indian dishes. They are ground into a powder and folded into the *loyah* (ball of dough filled with grounded or powdered seasoned split peas) to make dhalpuri roti, a favorite of Caribbean people among all ethnic groups.

Split peas are used in a variety of ways. They are great for soups, puree half of the cooked peas for a creamier texture. Yellow split peas are most often used to prepare *dal* in Guyana, Suriname, Mauritius, South Africa, Trinidad and Tobago and Fiji. Referred to as simply *dal*, it is prepared similar to *dals* found in India, but also may be used in a variety of other recipes.

Legumes, Nuts and Seeds

Nutritional Criteria	Summary of Ratings									
	Chickpeas	Red peas	Lima Beans	Lentils	Pigeon peas	Cow peas	Broad beans	Peanuts	Pumpkin seeds	Green Split Peas
	1	2	3	4	5	6	7	8	9	10
High in Complex Carbohydrates	8	6	6	4	6	4	4	2	0	3
High in Dietary Fibre	10	10	10	8	10	8	10	8	6	10
Low in Saturated Fats	10	10	10	10	10	10	10	6	4	10
High in Monounsaturated Fats	2	0	0	0	0	0	0	8	6	0
High in Polyunsaturated Fats	4	0	0	0	0	0	0	4	6	0
High in Iron	8	8	8	8	8	10	6	6	6	2
Low in Sodium	10	10	10	10	10	10	10	10	10	10
High in Potassium	8	8	10	8	8	10	8	8	8	8
High in Calcium	2	4	4	2	4	4	4	4	2	0
High in Vitamin A	0	0	0	0	0	0	0	0	0	0
High in Vitamin C	4	2	0	2	0	0	4	0	0	1
High in Vitamin B_6	10	8	10	10	8	8	8	4	4	6
High in Folate	10	10	10	8	8	10	8	4	4	4
Phytochemicals	8	8	6	6	8	6	6	4	6	4

BIBLIOGRAPHY

Avery, T. (2020). *The History, Science, and Uses of Chickpeas*. Retrieved from https://toriavey.com/the-history-science-and-uses-of-chickpeas/

Chel-Guerrero, L., Dominguez M., Mario A., Martinez-Ayala, A., Dávila-Ortiz, Gloria & Betancur, D. (2012). Lima Bean (Phaseolus lunatus) Protein Hydrolysates with ACE-I Inhibitory Activity. *Food and Nutrition Sciences. 03.* 10.4236/fns.2012.34072.

Flippone, P.T. (2020). *The History and Origin of Lentils*. Retrieved from https://www.thespruceeats.com/history-of-lentils-1807624 (Accessed April 8, 2020).

Heuzé V., Tran G., Sauvant D., Bastianelli D., Lebas F., 2015. Lima bean (Phaseolus lunatus)

Feedipedia, a programme by INRA, CIRAD, AFZ and FAO. http://www.feedipedia.org/node/267 Last updated on May 11, 2015, 14:31

Manonmani, D., Bhol, S. & Bosco, S. (2014). Effect of Red Kidney Bean (Phaseolus vulgaris L.) *Flour on Bread Quality*. OALib. 01. 1–6. 10.4236/oalib.1100366.

Rasool, S., Abdel, L. & Ahmad, P. (2015). Chickpea. 10.1002/9781118917091.ch4.

Shehzad, A. & Chander, Umer & Sharif, Mian & Rakha, Allah & Ansari, Anam & Shuja, Muhammad. (2015). *Nutritional, functional and health promoting attributes of red kidney beans; A Review.* 25. 235–246

Taylor C. Wallace, T.C., Murray, R. & Zelman K.M. (2016). The Nutritional Value and Health Benefits of Chickpeas and Hummus. 8, 766; doi:10.3390/nu8120766

United States Department of Agriculture National Agricultural Library. Lima Beans. Retrieved from https://agritrop.cirad.fr/582485/7/ID582485_ENG.pdf

Whitbread, D. (2020). Top 10 Beans and Legumes Highest in Protein https://www.myfooddata.com/articles/beans-legumes-highest-protein.php

5 | FOODS FROM ANIMALS

This group includes all foods which are either animal parts e.g. meat, fish or foods which are produced by animals e.g. animal milk, eggs. Apart from milk, foods from animals are generally high in protein, vary in fat content and do not contain appreciable amounts of carbohydrates. Milk is the only food from animals which will contribute a significant amount of carbohydrates to the diet. As a food group, they are also good sources of B vitamins and iron.

The global demand for meat is mounting. Over the last few decades meat production has more than quadrupled. The consumption of meat often parallels the consumption of fat. Questions continue to be raised about the risk of consuming fats to public health. The negative aspects of saturated fat have also come under scrutiny. Robust research will continue to provide more definitive information on the attributable risks of these fats. This is critical to formulate dietary guidelines for the general public. Meat is a primary source of dietary saturated fat, traditionally known as a main risk factor for cardiovascular disease. Obesity, diabetes, and colorectal cancer risks are also linked to higher meat consumption, mainly due to the relatively high overall saturated fat content of meat. Animal meat also contains several bioactive substances, such as creatine, taurine and cholesterol. What is clear is that the risks of excess meat consumption often outweigh the potential benefits. Based on current evidence it is safe to conclude that low consumption of saturated fats can reduce the risk of adverse health outcomes. Further, production and consumption of healthier meat products can also reduce these risks. Benefits can be achieved by promoting and consuming fish, which contains healthier fatty acids and less saturated fats than red meat.

Meats and poultry should be handled carefully to prevent cross contamination. They should be cooked well to prevent food borne illnesses. If these foods will not be used immediately, they should be properly wrapped and can be kept frozen for an extended period. Date labelling can be useful.

RANK #1 – LEAN CHICKEN

Nutritional Criteria	Rating
High in Complex Carbohydrates	0
High in Dietary Fibre	0
Low in Cholesterol	★★★★★★
Low in Saturated Fats	★★★★★★★★
High in Monounsaturated Fats	★★★★
High in Polyunsaturated Fats	★★★★★
High in Iron	★★
Low in Sodium	★★★★★★
High in Potassium	★★★★
High in Calcium	0
High in Vitamin A	0
High in Vitamin C	0
High in Vitamin B$_6$	★★★★★★★★
High in Folate	★★
Zoochemicals	★★★

LEAN CHICKEN

Scientific name: *Gallus gallus domesticus*

Origin and Background

Most of today's chicken is a descendant of the Red Jungle Fowl from Southeast Asia. The Red Jungle Fowl is believed to have been first domesticated around 2000 BC in India. Chicken that is prepared for consumption is described as 'dressed'. This means that all feathers, the head, neck, feet, and internal organs have been removed. The neck, liver, kidney, and gizzard are sometimes packaged and placed inside the dressed chicken. Chicken parts, including the feet, are also available for sale.

Varieties

There are over 1600 different recognized chicken breeds worldwide. Produced commercially, chickens are categorized in the following ways:

- *Broiler/Fryer* – about 7 weeks old and considered to be a young chicken. These are tender and can be cooked using any method. Weight is usually 2.5lbs to 4lbs and is the most widely available.
- *Rock Cornish Game Hen* – a small broiler/fryer weighing 1lb to 2lbs; usually stuffed and roasted whole or roasted without stuffing.
- *Roaster* – a young chicken between 8 to 12 weeks of age. When dressed, it usually weighs at least 5lbs. It is usually roasted whole and yields more meat per pound than a broiler-fryer; usually roasted whole.
- *Capons* – surgically unsexed male chickens between 16 weeks to 8 months old. They usually weigh 4lbs to 7lbs. The meat is tender and light; usually roasted.
- *Stewing/Baking Hen* – a laying hen usually aged 10 months to 1.5 years old. The meat is less tender than young chickens. It is best when cooked with moisture such as stewing.
- *Cock or Rooster* – a mature male chicken with coarse skin and tough dark meat; requires long, moist cooking.

Health and Dietary Benefits

Chicken is a main and almost a daily component of the omnivore's diet. It is usually accompanied by at least a Staple food.

Chicken provides high quality protein that the body can use easily. It is also low in fat, most of which is unsaturated and contained in the skin (which can be removed if desired). This makes it an excellent addition to the diet, once prepared in healthy ways. Chicken soup is widely used in the treatment of colds, flu, and fever.

Preparation and Culinary Uses

Chicken is very versatile and can be cooked in many ways. Chicken is usually seasoned or marinated in advance of cooking. Common seasonings include various herbs and spices e.g. thyme, scallion, peppers, garlic, onion, salt. Culturally-specific dishes may add turmeric, ginger, curry powder, jerk seasoning etc.

The fleshy parts of chicken are usually prepared by frying, baking, barbecuing, grilling, or stewing. It can also be used to make soups, pies/casseroles, sandwiches, wraps, salads, and stews. In the Caribbean, it is also an ingredient in many one-pot dishes e.g. pelau, cook-up. It is also popular as appetisers or snacks e.g. chicken tenders, chicken drumsticks and chicken wings.

Other Uses

Chicken excreta is sometimes added to soil and/or other items to make manure.

RANK #2 – SNAPPER

Nutritional Criteria	Rating
High in Complex Carbohydrates	0
High in Dietary Fibre	0
Low in Cholesterol	✮✮✮✮✮✮
Low in Saturated Fats	✮✮✮✮✮✮✮✮✮
High in Monounsaturated Fats	✮✮
High in Polyunsaturated Fats	✮✮✮
High in Iron	0
Low in Sodium	✮✮✮✮✮✮
High in Potassium	✮✮✮
High in Calcium	0
High in Vitamin A	0
High in Vitamin C	0
High in Vitamin B_6	✮✮✮✮✮✮
High in Folate	0
Zoochemicals	✮✮✮✮

SNAPPER

Scientific name: *Lutjanus campechanus*

Origin and Background

The snapper is a tropical and sub-tropical fish, harvested mainly from the waters of the Gulf of Mexico, the Caribbean and the South Atlantic. Though largely marine, the snapper is sometimes found feeding in fresh water. The snapper may grow up to 30 lbs and 3 feet in length. The skin is scaly. The meat is white and considered to be firm in texture with a mild or delicate taste.

Varieties

There are about 113 species of snapper. Seventeen (17) types are usually harvested from the waters mentioned above. Two common varieties are the red snapper and the yellowtail snapper.

The adult red snapper is bright red with a pale-coloured belly. The iris of the adult red snapper is also bright red.

Health and Dietary Benefits

Snapper is an excellent source of vitamin B_6 which is important for strengthening the immune system. It is also a good source of potassium which is important for blood pressure regulation and muscle function.

Preparation and Culinary Uses

Snapper is used as the main part of the meal for persons who consume fish.

It is often prepared whole. Common preparation methods are frying, roasting, steaming or stewing. A preparation of pickled seasonings such as onions, scotch bonnet peppers, pimentos, and vegetables such as carrot is sometimes used to garnish fried fish for a dish known as escoveitched fish, a Jamaican favourite. This is also enjoyed especially by other Caribbean peoples. Because of its firm flesh, snapper can also be grilled and baked. Snapper retains flavour well from marinades and seasonings.

Fresh snapper is ideally purchased as the last errand and should be kept cold during commute. It should be stored in the coldest part of the refrigerator and used within two days. Frozen snapper should be used within six months. When preparing for use, frozen snapper should be thawed in the refrigerator.

RANK #3 – SHARK

Nutritional Criteria	Rating
High in Complex Carbohydrates	0
High in Dietary Fibre	0
Low in Cholesterol	★★★★★★
Low in Saturated Fats	★★★★★★★★★
High in Monounsaturated Fats	★★
High in Polyunsaturated Fats	★
High in Iron	0
Low in Sodium	★★★★★★
High in Potassium	★★★
High in Calcium	0
High in Vitamin A	★★★★
High in Vitamin C	0
High in Vitamin B_6	★★★★★★
High in Folate	0
Zoochemicals	★★★

SHARK

Scientific name: *Selachimorpha sp.*

Origin and Background

Consumption of shark meat is not as popular in the Caribbean as it is in Eastern countries such as Japan, Korea, Australia, and some East African countries. Older shark meat tends to have a strong smell of ammonia the longer it remains unprepared. This odour can be alleviated by marinating the meat in saltwater, milk, vinegar, or lemon juice.

Varieties

The Black tip shark, fished from local waters, is commonly used in Trinidad and Tobago.

Health and Dietary Benefits

Shark meat is lean, with very little fat. In addition, most of the fat is unsaturated (polyunsaturated and monounsaturated). Unsaturated fats are associated with reduced risk of cardiovascular disease.

Preparation and Culinary Uses

In the Caribbean, the most popular preparation of shark is as a battered and deep-fried steak or fillet, sandwiched between a fried dough (bake). This bake and shark sandwich is sold as a popular Trinidadian street food or served at social gatherings. Inclusions of salad vegetables, pineapple and spicy local condiments enhances the palatability of this sandwich. Shark meat can also be stewed, curried, grilled, or used as a substitute for fish in local soup.

RANK #4 – EGG

Nutritional Criteria	Rating
High in Complex Carbohydrates	0
High in Dietary Fibre	0
Low in Cholesterol	☆☆
Low in Saturated Fats	☆☆
High in Monounsaturated Fats	☆☆☆
High in Polyunsaturated Fats	☆
High in Iron	☆☆☆☆
Low in Sodium	☆☆☆☆☆
High in Potassium	☆☆
High in Calcium	☆☆
High in Vitamin A	☆☆☆☆☆☆
High in Vitamin C	0
High in Vitamin B$_6$	☆☆☆☆
High in Folate	☆☆
Zoochemicals	☆☆☆☆☆

EGG

Scientific name: *Gallus gallus domesticus ovum*

Origin and Background

Chicken eggs, produced for commercial use, are unfertilised. Fresh eggs (in-shell) can spoil quickly at room temperature. Eggs should be refrigerated at a temperature 33–38°F or below to maintain their quality for a few weeks. Eggs in shell should not be frozen. Because the shell is porous, eggs should not be stored close to foods that have a strong odour. Prior to storing eggs, they can be wiped. Washing can remove the protective coating of the eggs and reduce shelf life. Eggs can, however, be washed immediately prior to use. This step will assist in reducing the risk of Salmonella infection.

Varieties

Eggs are sold in several different forms:

- In-shell (pasteurised or unpasteurised)
- Liquid
- Egg whites (liquid or powdered)

Eggs are generally available in three common sizes: extra-large, large and medium.

Health and Dietary Benefits

Eggs are a convenient source of about 18 important nutrients including protein, vitamins A, B_6 and iron. Compared with other food from animals, one medium egg provides the same amount of protein as one ounce of meat. It is an economical source of protein. Egg protein enhances the synthesis of skeletal muscles and can therefore be beneficial to persons undergoing athletic training. Egg protein does not contain purines, thus can be used by persons affected with gout. Eggs are a good source of vitamin B_{12} and egg yolks provide significant amounts of vitamins A and D. Egg yolk is also naturally high in dietary cholesterol. For healthy persons, the suggested dietary intake is less than 300 milligrams (mg) per day. One large egg has about 186 mg of cholesterol. To limit cholesterol intake the egg white alone can therefore be used.

Preparation and Culinary Uses

Only clean, previously uncracked eggs should be used. Eggs are versatile and very convenient because of the short cooking time required. They can be used whole, whites only or yolks only depending on the food being prepared. Some persons discard the yolks to increase their protein intake without also increasing dietary cholesterol and/or fat intake.

Eggs are mainly used as breakfast foods when they are served fried, scrambled, poached, boiled or as omelettes. Eggs are also important ingredient in baking, custards, puddings, meringues, and drinks such as eggnog. Egg dishes should not be kept at room temperature for more than one hour (including preparation and service time). Raw eggs should never be consumed. The mixing container (blender, bowl, mixer) or preparation tools should not be re-used before washing nor should the remainder of a mixture containing raw eggs be consumed.

Eggs cooked at too high of a temperature or for too long may develop a green cast. This is a result of reactions of sulphur and iron compounds from the egg. It is still safe to eat. Dried eggs (powdered) should be in a tightly sealed container and in a cool, dry environment, preferably below 50°F. Reconstitute only the amount that is required for immediate use. The shelf life varies for liquid, pasteurized eggs. Adhering to processor's guidelines is recommended. Hard boiled eggs, if not consumed should be refrigerated within two hours of cooking and consumed within 1 week.

Other Uses

Chicken eggs are sometimes used in protein treatments for strengthening hair. Egg whites have also been used to make facial masks as it is believed to tighten the skin.

RANK #5 – LEAN TURKEY

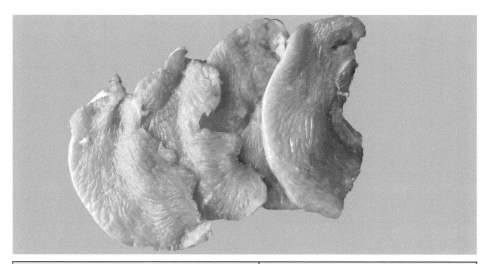

Nutritional Criteria	Rating
High in Complex Carbohydrates	0
High in Dietary Fibre	0
Low in Cholesterol	☆☆☆☆☆☆
Low in Saturated Fats	☆☆☆☆☆☆
High in Monounsaturated Fats	☆☆☆☆
High in Polyunsaturated Fats	☆☆☆☆☆
High in Iron	☆☆
Low in Sodium	☆☆☆☆☆☆
High in Potassium	☆☆☆☆
High in Calcium	0
High in Vitamin A	0
High in Vitamin C	0
High in Vitamin B_6	☆☆☆☆☆☆
High in Folate	0
Zoochemicals	☆☆☆

LEAN TURKEY

Scientific name: *Meleagris sp.*

Origin and Background

The domesticated turkey is popularly and traditionally consumed as a Thanksgiving and Christmas menu item in North America. Its consumption in the Caribbean continues to increase especially at Christmas. Turkeys have unique voices and are known to exhibit over 20 distinct vocalizations. They are also very sociable.

Varieties

Hen vs Tom: Hen (female) and Tom (male) turkeys are sold. The Hens usually weigh less, with smaller bones and more edible portions than the Tom turkey. The texture of the meat is usually determined by age and not sex.

Wild vs Farm Raised: Wild turkeys are sometimes consumed and usually have more dark meat than farm raised turkeys. The taste is also described as being more gamey.

Basted/Self-Basted: Dressed turkey labelled as basted or self-basted means that it has been marinated or injected with butter or another edible fat, broth, stock or water and spices and flavour enhancers.

Most turkeys sold for consumption are between 4 and 6 months old. Turkey is sold whole and dressed, ground, or in prepared slices as cold cuts.

Health and Dietary Benefits

Turkey meat is lean, with a low proportion of fat. Like other types of poultry, turkey is a main source of protein. It is also used in salads and sandwiches. Minced turkey is currently promoted as a lean alternative to ground beef.

Preparation and Culinary Uses

Turkey is like chicken in methods of preparation, however, if care is not taken it may become dry. Turkey is ideally suited for sandwiches. It can be roasted, fried, broiled, boiled, barbecued, grilled, and even smoked to be used as a substitute for bacon or ham (pork).

RANK #6 – SKIM MILK

Nutritional Criteria	Rating
High in Complex Carbohydrates	0
High in Dietary Fibre	0
Low in Cholesterol	★★★★★★★☆
Low in Saturated Fats	★★★★★★★★★☆
High in Monounsaturated Fats	0
High in Polyunsaturated Fats	0
High in Iron	0
Low in Sodium	★★★★★★
High in Potassium	★★
High in Calcium	★★★★
High in Vitamin A	★★
High in Vitamin C	0
High in Vitamin B$_6$	★★
High in Folate	0
Zoochemicals	★★★★

SKIM MILK

Other common name: Non-fat milk.

Origin and Background

Milk with very little fat is called skim milk. Milk has probably been consumed for 8,000–10,000 years since the domestication of the first cows called Aurochs. Milk is produced by the lacteal glands of cows. It is obtained by fully or partially milking the cows. Milk for human consumption may come from other animals such as goats and sheep. However, the most widely used animal milk is cow's milk. All commercially produced milk is pasteurised. This means that it is heated to high temperature to kill potentially harmful pathogens, then cooled rapidly to prevent the breakdown of its nutrients. The proteins from milk – casein and whey protein are sometimes isolated and sold as supplements and used mainly by persons who need to increase their protein intake.

Varieties

There are a few variations of cow's milk, produced to fit the expanding needs of consumers:

- Whole milk (about 3.5% fat)
- Low fat (less than 1.5% fat)
- Fat free/ skim (less than 0.15% fat)
- Lactose free

The different types of milk may be sold in an enriched form (added vitamin D) or they may be flavoured. Milk is available in liquid, powdered or evaporated forms. Condensed milk is also available.

Lactose free milk is the same as any of the above variations except for the lactose content. Lactose is a type of sugar found in milk products that can be difficult for some people to digest.

Health and Dietary Benefits

Cow's milk is an important source of calcium, high quality protein and vitamin D for persons who choose to consume it and who are not lactose intolerant. Condensed milk is not nutritionally comparable to cow's milk as it is significantly sweetened. Lactose free milk is suitable for persons who are lactose intolerant, but not for people with dairy allergy or those avoiding dairy for other reasons.

Preparation and Culinary Uses

Cow's milk is widely consumed in many ways. It is frequently consumed on its own, flavoured, or combined with other ingredients to make beverages. Milk is used as a complement to breakfast cereals, added to hot beverages such as coffee or tea, and cold beverages such as smoothies and shakes. Milk is also a key ingredient in various dough recipes, cakes and other pastries and creamy soups and sauces. Common by-products are butter, cheese, and yogurt.

Liquid milk is often sold in an aseptic paper package lined with plastic (Brand name: tetra-pak) which allows it to be shelf stable before opening, after which, it must be refrigerated. In some countries milk is still sold in plastic bags. These must be refrigerated even before use. Powdered milk has a much longer shelf life since it is in the dried form. According to the USDA, unopened powdered milk can be stored indefinitely. Condensed milk has a long shelf life.

Other Uses

Because of the lactic acid present in cow's milk, it is sometimes used in skin care as facial masks and baths.

RANK #7 – LEAN BEEF

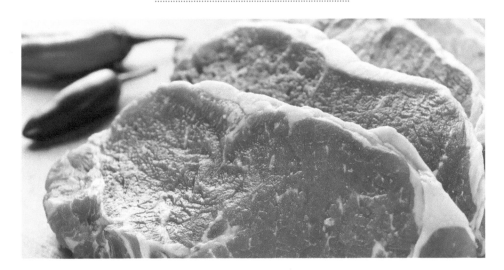

Nutritional Criteria	Rating
High in Complex Carbohydrates	0
High in Dietary Fibre	0
Low in Cholesterol	✮✮✮✮✮✮
Low in Saturated Fats	✮✮✮✮
High in Monounsaturated Fats	✮✮✮✮
High in Polyunsaturated Fats	✮
High in Iron	✮✮✮✮✮✮
Low in Sodium	✮✮✮✮✮✮
High in Potassium	✮✮✮✮
High in Calcium	0
High in Vitamin A	0
High in Vitamin C	0
High in Vitamin B$_6$	✮✮✮✮✮✮
High in Folate	0
Zoochemicals	✮

LEAN BEEF

Scientific name: *Bos taurus*

Origin and Background

About 10,000 years ago, cows were domesticated from wild varieties in India and Europe. The Anglo-Saxon *"cow"* became the French *"boeuf"*, which became *"beef"*. Beef is the flesh of adult cattle. It is the third most widely consumed meat after chicken and pork. In the Caribbean and around the world the beef of cow is the norm. The beef from buffalo is eaten in Asia and America.

Beef from grass-fed cows have more healthy nutrients than beef from grain-fed cows. Grass fed cows are common in the Caribbean. The fat in beef adds flavor but also adds significant amounts of calories. Lean beef has much less fat – less than 10%. Fresh beef must be stored in the refrigerator (below 4°C) to delay deterioration and decomposition. Always store raw meat below, never above, other cooked or ready-to-eat products.

Varieties

The two most recognized and well-known varieties of cows are the Holstein cow (known for her black-and-white spots) and the Jersey cow (varies from very light grey to a very dark fawn or black).

Beef is categorized according to the part of the cow from which it is cut. For example, shank is beef cut from the leg of the cow and the chuck is cut from the shoulder. The round is from the rear while the brisket is from the breast of the cow. The loin is cut from the back and the sirloin is close to the loin. Different cuts will have different textures and flavours.

Health and Dietary Benefits

Fresh, lean beef can be recommended as part of a healthy diet. Beef is exceptionally rich in high-quality protein, vitamins, and minerals. It may therefore improve muscle growth and maintenance, as well as exercise performance. The risk of iron deficiency anemia is also reduced because it is a rich source of iron. Processed beef is often high in both sodium and saturated fats. High consumption of processed and overcooked beef has been linked to an increased risk of heart disease and cancer. Foods such as cured beef, salami, sausages, and hot dogs should therefore be limited in the diet.

Preparation and Culinary Uses

Beef is usually eaten as roasts, ribs, or steaks, stews and in soups. The most appropriate cooking methods will depend on the cut of beef which is selected. Beef is also commonly ground or minced. Patties made of ground beef are popular in Jamaica. Hamburgers made from minced beef are popular across the Caribbean.

Other Uses

Many Indian religions do not appreciate killing cattle and eating beef. Cows have a sacred status and are considered to provide sustenance for families. They are integral to the landscape.

RANK #8 – LEAN PORK

Nutritional Criteria	Rating
High in Complex Carbohydrates	0
High in Dietary Fibre	0
Low in Cholesterol	☆☆☆☆☆☆
Low in Saturated Fats	☆☆☆
High in Monounsaturated Fats	☆☆☆
High in Polyunsaturated Fats	☆☆☆☆
High in Iron	☆☆☆
Low in Sodium	☆☆☆☆☆☆
High in Potassium	☆☆☆
High in Calcium	☆
High in Vitamin A	0
High in Vitamin C	0
High in Vitamin B$_6$	☆☆☆☆☆☆
High in Folate	0
Zoochemicals	☆

LEAN PORK

Scientific name: *Sus scrofa*

Origin and Background

Pork is the meat of the domestic pig. Globally, it is the most frequently consumed red meat. In some religious groups such as Seventh Day Adventist, Islam, Judaism and Rastafarianism it is forbidden. In fact, pork is even illegal in many Islamic countries.

Varieties

There are dozens of pig breeds in various countries. Popular ones are Landrace, Duroc, Berkshire, Chester and spotted. They distinguish themselves by the size of the breed, their colour, the length of the body and the texture of their hair.

Health and Dietary Benefits

Pork is a rich source of high-quality protein and micronutrients. As such lean pork can be a tasty addition to diet as it may improve exercise performance and promote muscle growth and maintenance. Pork is also a good source of many vitamins and minerals, including thiamine, zinc, vitamin B_{12}, vitamin B_6, niacin, phosphorus, and iron. It is also high in oleic acid, which is a monounsaturated fat that is readily available for use by the body. These nutrients play important positive roles in body functions.

Pork, however, contains artery-clogging cholesterol and saturated fat which can contribute to obesity and chronic diseases. Further, consumption of both undercooked and overcooked pork should be avoided. Overcooked pork may contain carcinogenic substances. In short, moderate consumption of properly prepared lean pork can be a useful part of a healthy diet.

Preparation and Culinary Uses

In the Caribbean, apart from raw and minimally processed pork it is common to find products such as smoked pork, ham, bacon, and sausages. Pork is especially prone to infections so cooking it to the correct temperature is vital for preventing parasitic infections and reducing the risk of foodborne illness caused by strains of bacteria. Despite the decline in the incidence of infections due to improved hygiene, guidelines and laws in recent decades, the proper preparation and thorough cooking of pork are still crucial. Pork should be handled and stored properly to ensure safety. Raw pork should be exposed to unsafe temperatures for as short a time as possible. Raw pork can be stored in a refrigerator for several days, depending on the type of cut. It should be kept below 4°C to prevent bacteria, which causes foodborne illness, from growing quickly. Pork should be cooked to at least 63°C. This allows the meat to maintain its moisture and flavour without drying it out.

Other Uses

Several medicines such as tablets, injections, capsules, creams, mixtures, and vaccines contain gelatin which is a product derived from pork and beef.

RANK #9 – TILAPIA

Nutritional Criteria	Rating
High in Complex Carbohydrates	0
High in Dietary Fibre	0
Low in Cholesterol	✭✭✭✭✭✭
Low in Saturated Fats	✭✭✭✭✭✭✭✭
High in Monounsaturated Fats	0
High in Polyunsaturated Fats	0
High in Iron	0
Low in Sodium	✭✭✭✭✭✭
High in Potassium	✭✭✭✭
High in Calcium	0
High in Vitamin A	0
High in Vitamin C	0
High in Vitamin B$_6$	✭✭
High in Folate	0
Zoochemicals	✭✭

TILAPIA

Scientific name: *Oreochromis niloticus*

Origin and Background

Historical investigation shows that Tilapia may have been cultivated as far back as 4000 years ago in Egypt. Worldwide distribution bloomed in the period from the 1940s to the 1980s, with the Nile Tilapia becoming the popular variety. Tilapia was introduced to many Caribbean countries as part of an aquaculture programme. Tilapia can be grown in freshwater ponds and compete well with other options when consumer choice is considered.

Varieties

There are primarily three commercial species of tilapia. These are:

1. Nile tilapia
2. Blue tilapia
3. Mozambique tilapia (hybrid of the Nile and Blue varieties)

Commercially produced tilapia are usually male since they grow twice as fast as females.

Health and Dietary Benefits

Farm raised tilapia have a high ratio of omega-6 to omega-3 fatty acids. Tilapia is high in protein, low in fat and provides an appreciable amount of potassium and phosphorous to the diet.

Preparation and Culinary Uses

Tilapia is commonly processed into boneless, skinless fillets and are usually fried, battered or unbattered. Other food preparation methods can be explored.

Other Uses

Tilapia can be used to control algae and mosquito population in ponds and other freshwater enclosures.

RANK # 10 – LEAN GOAT

Nutritional Criteria	Rating
High in Complex Carbohydrates	0
High in Dietary Fibre	0
Low in Cholesterol	★★★★★★
Low in Saturated Fats	★★★★
High in Monounsaturated Fats	0
High in Polyunsaturated Fats	0
High in Iron	★★
Low in Sodium	★★★★★★
High in Potassium	★★
High in Calcium	0
High in Vitamin A	0
High in Vitamin C	0
High in Vitamin B$_6$	0
High in Folate	0
Zoochemicals	★

LEAN GOAT

Scientific name: *Capra aegagrus hircus*

Origin and Background

Cave art between 10,000 and 20,000 years ago suggest that goats may have been the earliest domesticated animals. Seventy five percent of all the goats in the world can be found in developing countries.

Varieties

There are over 450 million goats around the world comprising 210 breeds. The three common groups are: domestic goats which are raised and bred on farms, wild goats which are ubiquitous and mountain goats which are also wild but occupy mountainous areas.

Health and Dietary Benefits

Goat meat is generally lean. Compared to whole, dressed chicken, goat meat has considerably less cholesterol, less total fat, and less saturated fat. It also provides more iron.

Preparation and Culinary Uses

The meat from male goats is lighter in colour and lower in fat compared to the meat from female goats. The meat from female goats is usually preferred for steaks and chops since it is more tender. Cubed goat meat can retain its high quality in the freezer for up to four months. For larger cuts, quality can be retained up to nine months.

Goat meat, especially of an older goat, may be tough. Using a pressure cooker shortens cooking time and helps to tenderize the meat. Alternatively, the meat may be braised in a small amount of liquid in a tightly covered pot.

Goat meat is usually served along with complementing staple foods. Goat meat is popularly curried or stewed but may also be grilled, baked, fried or barbecued. Stews are commonly served with rice and is popularly used as a filling for roti. In Jamaica, the head of the goat is used to make soup called Manish Water.

Other Uses

Goats are also raised for wool. The manure is often used for fertilizer. Goats pull carts in some countries. They are also used for research models in biological studies.

Foods from Animals

Nutritional Criteria	Summary of Ratings									
	Lean Chicken	Snapper	Shark	Egg	Lean Turkey	Skim Milk	Lean Beef	Lean Pork	Tilapia	Lean Goat
	1	2	3	4	5	6	7	8	9	10
High in Complex Carbohydrates	0	0	0	0	0	0	0	0	0	0
High in Dietary Fibre	0	0	0	0	0	0	0	0	0	0
Low in Cholesterol	6	6	6	2	6	8	6	6	6	6
Low in Saturated Fats	8	9	9	2	6	10	4	4	8	4
High in Monounsaturated Fats	4	2	2	3	4	0	4	4	0	0
High in Polyunsaturated Fats	5	4	1	1	5	0	1	5	0	0
High in Iron	2	0	0	4	2	0	6	4	0	2
Low in Sodium	6	6	6	4	6	6	6	6	6	6
High in Potassium	4	4	3	2	4	2	4	4	4	2
High in Calcium	0	0	0	2	0	4	0	1	0	0
High in Vitamin A	0	0	4	6	0	2	0	0	0	0
High in Vitamin C	0	0	0	0	0	0	0	0	0	0
High in Vitamin B_6	8	6	6	4	6	2	6	6	2	0
High in Folate	2	0	0	2	0	0	0	0	0	0
Zoochemicals	3	4	3	5	3	4	1	1	2	1

BIBLIOGRAPHY

American Egg Board. Egg Storage & Handling. Retrieved from: https://www.aeb.org/foodservice/egg-safety-handling/egg-storage-handlin

FAO. Retrieved from: http://www.fao.org/fishery/culturedspecies/Oreochromis_niloticus/en)

Florida Department of Agriculture and Consumer Services, Retrieved from: https://www.freshfromflorida.com/Consumer-Resources/Buy-Fresh-From-Florida/Seafood-Products/Red-Snapper accessed April 28, 2019

Mayo Clinic, Eggs: Are they good or bad for my cholesterol?

Michigan State University, Extension Bulletin E3232, November 2014, Handling, Using & Storing Poultry

Miranda. J.M., Anton, X., Redondo-Valbuena, C., Roca-Saavedra, P., Rodriquez, J.A.,

Lamas, A., Franco, C.M., & Cepeda, A. (2015). Egg and Egg-Derived Foods: Effects on Human Health and Use as Functional Foods, Nutrients. 2015 Jan; 7(1): 706–729. PMCID: PMC4303863, Published online 2015 Jan 20. doi: 10.3390/nu7010706 PMID: 25608941

Molt, M. (2006). Food for Fifty: Food Product Information, 12th edition Pearson Prentice Hall.

Singh, R. K., Chang, H. W., Yan, D., Lee, K. M., Ucmak, D., Wong, K., Abrouk, M., Farahnik, B., Nakamura, M., Zhu, T. H., Bhutani, T., & Liao, W. (2017). Influence of diet on the gut microbiome and implications for human health. Journal of translational medicine, 15(1), 73. https://doi.org/10.1186/s12967-017-1175-y

University of Illinois Extension, Turkey for the Holidays. Retrieved from http://extension.illinois.edu/turkey/selection.cfm

United States Department of Agriculture (USDA) (2019). Food Safety and Inspection Service, Turkey From Farm to Table. Retrieved from https://www.fsis.usda.gov/wps/portal/fsis/topics/food-safety-education/get-answers/food-safety-fact-sheets/poultry-preparation/food-safety-of-turkeyfrom-farm-to-table/ct_index, United States Department of Agriculture- Agricultural Research Service, National Nutrient Database for Standard Reference Legacy Release, Retrieved from https://ndb.nal.usda.gov/ndb/foods/show/15262?fgcd=&manu=&format=&count=&max=25&offset=&sort=default&order=asc&qlookup=tilapia&ds=SR&qt=&qp=&qa=&qn=&q=&ing=

United States Department of Agriculture (USDA). (2019). Food Safety and Inspection Service, Goat from Farm to Table, https://www.fsis.usda.gov/wps/portal/fsis/topics/food-safety-education/get-answers/food-safety-fact-sheets/meat-preparation/goat-from-farm-to-table/ct_index, Accessed 07 May 2019 BMJ 2015;351:h3978 doi: 10.1136/bmj.h3978

United States Department of Agriculture (USDA). (2019). Food Safety and Inspection Service, Chicken From Farm to Table, https://www.fsis.usda.gov/wps/portal/fsis/topics/food-safety-education/get-answers/food-safety-fact-sheets/poultry-preparation/chicken-from-farm-to-table/ct_index, United States Department of Agriculture-Agricultural Research Service, National Nutrient Database for Standard Reference Legacy Release, https://ndb.nal.usda.gov/ndb/foods/show/15095?fgcd=&manu=&format=&count=&max=25&offset=&sort=default&order=asc&qlookup=shark&ds=SR&qt=&qp=&qa=&qn=&q=&ing=

US Department of Health and Human Services, US Food and Drug Administration, CRF Code of Federal Regulations Title 21, Part 131 Milk and Cream https://www.accessdata.fda.gov/scripts/cdrh/cfdocs/cfcfr/CFRSearch.cfm?fr=131.110

United States Department of Agriculture (USDA). (2014). Chicken from Farm to Table. Retrieved from https://www.fsis.usda.gov/wps/wcm/connect/ad74bb8d-1dab-49c1-b05e-390a74ba7471/Chicken_from_Farm_to_Table.pdf?MOD=AJPERES

Velente L, 2017, Why was the first cow milked in the first place? Retrieved from https://medium.com/@lanavalente/the-origins-of-milk-why-did-the-first-cow-milker-milk-the-cow-c41e8ef761d6

6 FATS AND OILS

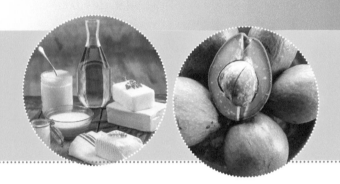

Fats and oils are important to everyone's diet regardless of age. Most fats and oils are good sources of vitamins A and D. Some foods may also be enriched if commercially prepared and depending on the source (e.g. dairy source), they may contribute calcium to the diet. Fats and oils are also important in the formation of hormones, cushioning and protecting parts of the body e.g. palms, soles of feet, buttocks; maintaining the integrity of nerve fibres; a source of energy for activities of long duration, and during periods of deprivation.

Three popular plant foods that are highly ranked have often received negative health ratings in the Caribbean. These are the products of coconut, avocado and ackee mainly because of their well-established fat (fatty acid) content. Over the years, research has shown that the purported health risks are unfounded simply because all fats are not equal. The concern is created because fat is the most concentrated source of energy in the diet and obesity is the most important underlying cause of death in the region. Further, specific fatty acids have been linked to cancers and other chronic diseases.

The ingestion of fat must be placed in the context of use, quantity, and type. Ultimately, it must be recognized that plant fats have a high fat content, and the excess energy will be stored as fat which is a major contributor to obesity and non-communicable diseases, the most important health problems in the Caribbean. However, there is no reason to avoid these low-cost, commonly available, and popular foods. These plant fats should therefore be included in national dietary guidelines. The important facts are that saturated fats should not make up more than 10% of the total calories in the diet. Monounsaturated and polyunsaturated fats, when used as a replacement for saturated fats in the diet (in healthy quantities) help to decrease risk of developing cardiovascular diseases and help to decrease the risk of stroke and heart attack. Trans fats should be avoided. The fats and oils on the following pages were ranked according to the types of fats they contain, the proportions and other nutrients which may be present.

RANK #1 – AVOCADO

Nutritional Criteria	Rating
High in Complex Carbohydrates	0
High in Dietary Fibre	✮✮✮✮✮✮
Low in Saturated Fats	✮✮✮✮✮✮
High in Monounsaturated Fats	✮✮✮✮✮✮✮
High in Polyunsaturated Fats	✮✮✮✮✮✮
Low in Cholesterol	✮✮✮✮✮✮✮✮✮✮
High in Iron	0
Low in Sodium	✮✮✮✮✮✮✮✮✮✮
High in Potassium	✮✮✮✮
High in Calcium	✮
High in Vitamin A	✮✮
High in Vitamin C	✮✮✮✮
High in Vitamin B$_6$	✮✮✮✮
High in Folate	✮✮✮✮
Phytochemicals	✮✮✮✮

AVOCADO

Scientific name: *Persea americana*
Other Common Name(s): Zaboca/Zabooka/Zaboka, Avocado Pear.

Origin and Background

Fossil evidence suggests that avocados existed millions of years ago. Evidence supports three recognised domestic varieties. These are Mexican, Guatemalan and West Indian. The English word 'avocado' was first documented in the 1696 index of Jamaican Plants by Hans Sloane.

These varieties were introduced to various parts of the world, including the United States and Europe. The main producers of the world's avocado supply are Mexico, Chile, Dominican Republic, Indonesia, United States, Australia, South Africa, and Israel.

Varieties

Today, there are two flowering types – Cultivar A and Cultivar B. There are several varieties within each cultivar. The key cultivars of economic importance in the Caribbean region include Pollock, Lula, and Simmonds.

Pollock is oblong to pear shaped and can weigh up to 2.27 kg (5 lbs). The seed is loose in the cavity and the tree bears from early July to August or October.

Lula is a Guatemalan and Mexican cross hybrid. The fruit is pear shaped, sometimes with a neck, and the seed is tight within cavity. The tree bears between mid-November to December.

Simmonds is oblong (oval) pear shaped with the seed tight within cavity. It bears between mid-July to mid-September.

The shapes of these cultivars vary from tall, upright trees to widely spreading forms with multiple branches and heights ranging between 4–15 metres (13–60 feet).

Avocados brown easily after peeling. To avoid this, they should be used quickly. If that is not possible, lemon or lime juice can be used to coat the exposed areas to prevent browning.

Interestingly, the avocado was considered a hazard in recent years. Anecdotally, there was an increase in patients visiting emergency rooms in the United States for treatment of 'avocado hand'. This condition was so called because the patients all received severe injury to their hands from a knife being used to remove the avocado seed, to slice or to peel the avocado.

Health and Dietary Benefits

Avocado contains mainly unsaturated fats with oleic acid contributing 50–80% of lipids, depending on variety. The saturated fat content is about 14% (palmitic acid). In addition, avocado is sodium free and a good source of potassium and fibre. It is also a valuable antioxidant due to its vitamin A, C and E content. Further, avocado is not a source of dietary cholesterol. Rather, it lowers blood cholesterol, is rich in folic acid and vitamin K and as such can be a healthy option if used appropriately. Diets high in monounsaturated and poly unsaturated fats reduce development of metabolic diseases like Type 2 Diabetes and reduces likelihood of heart attacks and strokes.

Preparation and Culinary Uses

The avocado is usually consumed when ripe, but still firm. It is sliced and peeled or cut in a desired segment and the seed removed. The flesh can then be scooped out. Avocado is usually consumed either by itself, as a side dish with meals, or a salad ingredient. Because of its mild flavour, it is used in many different types of sandwiches, with other fillings or by itself. It can also be used in cake recipes as a substitute for vegetable oil, butter or shortening. When used in this way it adds nutrients and lightens the texture of the cake. Avocado is also used to make spreads, dips (guacamole), and can even be used as a base for smoothies. Its use has also become popular as a spread on toasted bread.

Other Uses

Avocado Oil is extracted and used for hair and skin care, either alone or in combination with other oils or butters.

RANK #2 – ACKEE

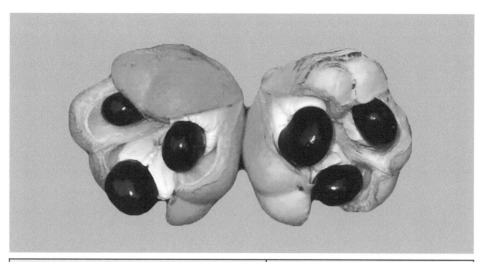

Nutritional Criteria	Rating
High in Complex Carbohydrates	0
High in Dietary Fibre	★★★☆
Low in Saturated Fats	★★★★★☆
High in Monounsaturated Fats	★★★★★☆
High in Polyunsaturated Fats	★☆
Low in Cholesterol	★★★★★★★★★☆
High in Iron	☆
Low in Sodium	★★★★★★★☆
High in Potassium	★★★☆
High in Calcium	★★★☆
High in Vitamin A	☆
High in Vitamin C	★★★☆
High in Vitamin B$_6$	☆
High in Folate	☆
Phytochemicals	★★

ACKEE

Scientific name: *Blighia sapida*
Other Common Name(s): achee, akee, Ackee apple, ayee

Origin and Background

The ackee was imported to the West Indies from West Africa, most likely on slave ships.

The fruit is most widely eaten in Jamaica. However, it has been gradually introduced to other Caribbean countries such as Trinidad and Tobago, Grenada, Antigua and Barbuda, and Barbados.

Varieties

There are two main types of ackee which can be identified by the colour of the aril (flesh): The Butter ackee is yellow and soft while the Cheese ackee is cream coloured and has a firmer texture. Ackee is available fresh or canned.

Health and Dietary Benefits

Ackee is mainly an unsaturated fat with a fatty acid composition that is of great significance to health outcomes. It was previously found that 51–58% of lipids in ackee contain mainly linoleic and stearic fatty acids. Additional research which used a more robust methodology, showed minor to undetectable levels of linoleic acid and 13% stearic acid. Importantly, however, the dominant lipid (55%) is oleic acid. Although the negative health consequences of linoleic and stearic acid are not compelling, oleic acid, in contrast, has a very positive effect on HDL/LDL cholesterol ratio and reduces the risk of chronic diseases and breast cancer. Ackee has additional health benefits through its protein content. It is also a good source of vitamins B and C, zinc, calcium and fibre.

Preparation and Culinary Uses

Ackee is most known as Jamaica's National Dish – Ackee and Saltfish and is also a popular part of vegetarian diets in Jamaica.

Ackee naturally contains a poisonous amino acid called hypoglycin. If consumed, it causes rapid drop in blood sugar and vomiting. Known as Jamaican Vomiting Sickness. To prevent this the following steps should be taken:

- Allow the ackee to fully ripen on the tree, that is, pods must fully open on their own.
- Remove the red fibre fully before cooking.
- Do not consume the water in which the ackee was boiled.

Ackee is boiled and then sautéed with seasonings. Fish or other meat is sometimes added e.g., saltfish, corned pork.

RANK #3 – CANOLA OIL

Nutritional Criteria	Rating
High in Complex Carbohydrates	0
High in Dietary Fibre	0
Low in Saturated Fats	★★★★★★★☆
High in Monounsaturated Fats	★★★★★★★★☆
High in Polyunsaturated Fats	★★★★★☆
Low in Cholesterol	★★★★★★★★★☆
High in Iron	0
Low in Sodium	★★★★★★★★★☆
High in Potassium	0
High in Calcium	0
High in Vitamin A	0
High in Vitamin C	0
High in Vitamin B$_6$	0
High in Folate	0
Phytochemicals	★★☆

CANOLA OIL

Scientific name: *Brassica napus*

Origin and Background

There is no plant that produces Canola oil. The name is derived from the words Canada and Ola which means oil. The oilseed was developed from the rapeseed using plant breeding techniques in Canada during the 1970s. Canola oil is simply a trade name for low-erucic acid oil from the rapeseed plant *Brassica napus*. To be called canola, the oilseed must meet recognised international standard, including that the oil should contain less than 2% erucic acid. Despite its origin, Canola oil has become the most popular cooking oil today.

Varieties

The types of seeds and how the oil is pressed/produced determines the grade of the oil. The main types are salad oil, expeller pressed, Non-GMO and Organic canola oil.

Health and Dietary Benefits

Canola oil contains the least amount of saturated fats of any edible oil. It is 93% mono-unsaturated and poly-unsaturated fats. Replacing saturated fats in the diet with unsaturated fats can decrease risk of type 2 diabetes and cardiovascular events.

Preparation and Culinary Uses

Canola oil and products are used for deep frying, baking and in sandwich spreads. It is also used in coffee whiteners and creamers. Canola oil is used to make margarine, salad oil and shortening.

Other Uses

Canola oil is used to make cosmetics, printing inks, suntan oils, oiled fabrics, plasticizers, plastic wraps, pesticides, and industrial lubricants. Research is being conducted to investigate application as diesel fuels and industrial oils.

RANK #4 – OLIVE OIL

Nutritional Criteria	Rating
High in Complex Carbohydrates	0
High in Dietary Fibre	0
Low in Saturated Fats	★ ★ ★ ★ ★ ☆
High in Monounsaturated Fats	★ ★ ★ ★ ★ ★ ★ ☆
High in Polyunsaturated Fats	★ ★ ★ ★ ★ ☆
Low in Cholesterol	★ ★ ★ ★ ★ ★ ★ ★ ☆
High in Iron	0
Low in Sodium	★ ★ ★ ★ ★ ★ ★ ★ ☆
High in Potassium	0
High in Calcium	0
High in Vitamin A	0
High in Vitamin C	0
High in Vitamin B$_6$	0
High in Folate	0
Phytochemicals	★ ☆

OLIVE OIL

Scientific name: *Olea europaea*
Other Common Name(s): Sweet oil

Origin and Background

Olive oil is produced from the olive fruit, a traditional crop in Mediterranean countries. The largest producers of olive oil are Spain, Greece, Italy, Turkey, Morocco, Syria, and Tunisia.

Varieties

Olive oil may be classified as extra virgin, virgin or refined. The definitions may differ depending on the country and their labelling standards or requirements.

- *Extra Virgin* olive oil is generally the highest grade of olive oil. It has undergone no refining and retains much of its flavour.
- *Virgin* olive oil is also unrefined but may not be as flavourful as the extra virgin type.
- *Refined* olive oil has been treated with mechanical filtering and may have a small amount of virgin olive oil added to improve the taste.

The quality of olive oil will deteriorate when exposed to light, air and/or heat. It should be used as quickly as possible, stored in a cool, dark place, and kept closed once not in use, to delay rancidity.

Health and Dietary Benefits

Olive oil is high in unsaturated fats. Therefore, replacing saturated fats in the diet with olive oil will reduce risk of developing NCDs such as type 2 diabetes and the likelihood of a stroke or heart attack.

Preparation and Culinary Uses

Extra Virgin olive oil is often used as salad dressing, added to foods which are eaten cold, and for sautéing. It is not suitable for deep frying or stewing.

Refined olive oil has a higher smoke point and can be used for deep frying.

Other Uses

Olive oil is used for the following:

- Body beauty
  - Hair and skin care – alone or as an ingredient in:
    - ▷ Shampoos and conditioners
    - ▷ Lotions
    - ▷ Moisturisers
    - ▷ Soaps
    - ▷ Exfoliant scrubs

- Religious ceremonies
- Lubricant for machinery

RANK #5 – SOFT MARGARINE

Nutritional Criteria	Rating
High in Complex Carbohydrates	0
High in Dietary Fibre	0
Low in Saturated Fats	✮✮✮✮✮✩
High in Monounsaturated Fats	✮✮✮✮✮✩
High in Polyunsaturated Fats	✮✮✮✮✮✩
Low in Cholesterol	✮✮✮✮✮✮✮✮✮✩
High in Iron	0
Low in Sodium	✮✮✮✮✮✩
High in Potassium	0
High in Calcium	0
High in Vitamin A	✮✮✮✩
High in Vitamin C	0
High in Vitamin B$_6$	0
High in Folate	0
Phytochemicals	0

SOFT MARGARINE

Other Common Name(s): Marge, Oleo, Oleomargarine

Origin and Background

Margarine is made with vegetable oils and water. It usually undergoes a process called hydrogenation to make it into a solid at room temperature. Margarine made from vegetable oils was engineered as a substitute for animal fats because of their lower saturated fat content. It can also be made from animal products (e.g. milk). However, the focus here is about those made from vegetable oils. Margarine may be kept for 3–4 months unopened, and 1–2 months opened. It should be kept refrigerated to maintain quality.

Varieties

Margarine can contain both plant and animal fats. It is available either as hard or soft margarine. Hard margarine is made from hydrogenated oil and is usually sold in sticks and blocks. Soft margarine usually comes in a tub, and spreads easily.

Health and Dietary Benefits

Plant sterol esters and stanol esters have been added to some margarines. These compounds are believed to lower risk of cardiovascular disease.

Preparation and Culinary Uses

Margarine is used as a spread and in baked products such as cakes, cookies, and other pastries. It is primarily a substitute for butter.

RANK #6 – COCONUT CREAM/OIL

Nutritional Criteria	Rating
High in Complex Carbohydrates	0
High in Dietary Fibre	★★
Low in Saturated Fats	★★★
High in Monounsaturated Fats	★★★★
High in Polyunsaturated Fats	★★
Low in Cholesterol	★★★★★★★★★★
High in Iron	★★★★
Low in Sodium	★★★★★★
High in Potassium	★★★★
High in Calcium	★
High in Vitamin A	0
High in Vitamin C	0
High in Vitamin B$_6$	★★
High in Folate	★★
Phytochemicals	★★

COCONUT – CREAM AND OIL

Scientific name: *Cocos nucifera*
Other Common Name(s): copra oil

Origin and Background

The coconut is a tree in the Palm family and grows in tropical and sub-tropical climates. Coconut cream and coconut oil are derived from the flesh of mature, dried coconuts. At this stage, the flesh or 'meat' is thick, white, and tough.

Coconut cream is traditionally made by grating the white kernel, to which running or hot water to the grated meat is pressed to release the creamy liquid. The chopped coconut kernel may also be processed in a high-speed blender with water, and this mixture strained and pressed. From these methods, and in a short time, the resulting liquid (coconut milk/cream) will settle to the top and can be skimmed off. Note that coconut milk is not comparable to animal milk and should therefore should not be used as a substitute. Coconut oil is made by gently heating the coconut milk. The oil fraction will separate and can be removed.

Varieties

Coconut cream is usually sold liquid or powdered. Brands differ mainly by country of origin, as all are made from the same plant.

There are several types of coconut oil on the market. Common labeling could include the terms Refined or Unrefined. Unrefined coconut oil may sometimes be referred to as pure, raw, or virgin coconut oil. Virgin coconut oil can be pure, like raw coconut oil, but raw coconut oil goes through the minimum amount of processing. Not all virgin is raw but all raw is virgin. The method of extraction also describes the oil.

Coconut oil may be classified as virgin or refined.

Virgin/Raw/Unrefined coconut oil is made using methods like the traditional cold-pressed methods. No heat is used. This oil is a firm, white butter that melts into a clear, fine oil. Modern process innovations involve the use of a centrifuge to separate the oil from the coconut milk. Virgin coconut oil has a distinct coconut flavour and smell.

Some of these oils may be labelled "Extra Virgin" but according to the USDA there is no difference between these alleged types.

Refined coconut oil is made by using a heated press to extract the oil from the dried kernel. It must be further heated and then filtered to remove contaminants and make it safe for consumption. Refined coconut oil does not retain the characteristic coconut smell or taste.

Coconut oil does not become rancid as quickly as some other oils. It can be stored for up to 6 months without a change in quality or flavour.

Health and Dietary Benefits

Coconut oil is a saturated fat, but unlike other oils and fats, about 40–50% of the fatty acid in coconut oil is lauric acid. Lauric acid offers unique properties related to its antiviral, antibacterial, and antiprotozoal functions. The combination of lauric, caprylic, oleic and capric fatty acids in coconut oil is a nutritional asset because these medium and short-chain fatty acids are useful in the treatment of certain digestive diseases.

Virgin coconut oil contains medium chain fatty acids (MCT) which speed up metabolism. Recent focus has been on the potential of coconut oil to elevate low-density ("bad") lipoprotein (LDL), but more importantly, it also raises the high-density("good") lipoprotein (HDL). What is noteworthy is that virgin coconut oil does not appear to adversely affect the critical HDL/LDL cholesterol ratio. Virgin coconut oil contains no cholesterol and is not hydrogenated.

Coconut cream is a good source of potassium and is low in sodium. Coconut oil may be effective in managing atopic dermatitis. There is no reason to exclude coconut oil from the Caribbean diet using the dietary guidelines related to saturated fat.

Preparation and Culinary Uses

Coconut cream has a sweet flavour and is used in many Caribbean dishes to create a rich and unique flavour. The main ingredient may be fish, meats, legumes, and staples in various combinations, e.g. mackerel run down, breadfruit oil down. Coconut cream is also added to some rice and peas dishes, and curries as another variation of curry sauce. Recently, coconut cream has found use as a base for vegan alternatives to traditional ice cream.

Coconut oil is a heat-stable cooking oil and is ideal for frying. It can also be used for sautéing and in baked goods. Hydrogenated coconut oil is an ingredient in many coffee creamers.

Other Uses

Coconut oil (refined or virgin) is utilised on its own or as part of formulations for hair and skin. It is beneficial for use in cosmetics, typically as a moisturizer, and in soaps.

RANK #7 — VEGETABLE SHORTENING

Nutritional Criteria	Rating
High in Complex Carbohydrates	0
High in Dietary Fibre	0
Low in Saturated Fats	☆
High in Monounsaturated Fats	☆☆☆☆☆☆☆☆☆
High in Polyunsaturated Fats	☆☆☆☆☆☆
Low in Cholesterol	☆☆☆☆☆☆☆☆☆
High in Iron	0
Low in Sodium	☆☆☆☆☆☆☆☆☆
High in Potassium	0
High in Calcium	0
High in Vitamin A	0
High in Vitamin C	0
High in Vitamin B$_6$	0
High in Folate	0
Phytochemicals	0

VEGETABLE SHORTENING

Other Common Name(s): Hydrogenated oil

Origin and Background

Vegetable shortening is made using various plant oils. It is considered a substitute for lard since it functions the same way but is lower in saturated fat. It is named shortening because it produces a crumbly texture in doughs during baking. This texture is also called 'short' since long strands of gluten are not formed. It does not require refrigeration and can last up to a year in an airtight container at room temperature. Vegetable shortening remains solid at room temperature, but vegetable oil does not.

Varieties

Vegetable shortening is usually made from palm, cottonseed or corn oils which are either hydrogenated or partially hydrogenated. Many brands are available.

Health and Dietary Benefits

Vegetable shortening which is fully hydrogenated vegetable oil becomes hard and is free of trans fat. Note that partial hydrogenation creates artificial trans fats, which have serious negative health effects. Vegetable shortening contains less saturated fat than butter or lard. While it is 100% fat, most of the fats are unsaturated. Vegetable shortening also provides vitamin K to the diet which is important in blood clotting and bone health. Vegetable shortening is highly processed and the health effects of this are still unknown.

Preparation and Culinary Uses

Useful in recipes which require pure fat. The high smoke point also makes it suitable for frying. Vegetable shortening is good for shortbreads, puff pastries, and pie crusts, and create a light texture.

Other Uses

Vegetable shortening is also used for the following:

1. To remove ink stains from skin

2. To remove gum from hair or fabric
3. To season cast iron cookware
4. To lubricate metal hinges

RANK #8 – LARD

Nutritional Criteria	Rating
High in Complex Carbohydrates	0
High in Dietary Fibre	0
Low in Saturated Fats	★★
High in Monounsaturated Fats	★★★★★★
High in Polyunsaturated Fats	★★★★
Low in Cholesterol	★★★★
High in Iron	0
Low in Sodium	★★★★★★★★★★
High in Potassium	0
High in Calcium	0
High in Vitamin A	0
High in Vitamin C	0
High in Vitamin B$_6$	0
High in Folate	0
Zoochemicals	0

LARD

Other Common Name(s): Leaf lard, tallow

Origin and Background

Lard is a by-product of pork production from pigs. It has been in use since the domestication of pigs for food. The fat from the pig is called lard in both its rendered and un-rendered form. Rendering is usually done by steaming, boiling or dry heat.

It is recommended that lard be stored in a cool dark place, and the container kept tightly shut.

Varieties

Types of lard differ in quality based on the parts of the pig from which the fat is taken.

1. **Flare fat** – produces the highest grade of lard called leaf lard. Flare fat is found deposited around the kidneys and inside the loin.
2. **Fatback** – this hard fat is taken from between the skin and muscle of the pig's back.
3. **Caul fat** – produces the lowest grade of lard. Caul fat is found around the digestive organs.

Health and Dietary Benefits

Over 50% of the fat in lard is unsaturated. Most of lard's monounsaturated fat is oleic acid, a heart-healthy essential fatty acid. Lard is also a good source of vitamin D.

Preparation and Culinary Uses

Lard is an ingredient in some patties, sausages, and flaky pastry crust. Its smoke point is high which makes it suitable for frying foods.

Other Uses

Rendered lard may be used in biofuels. Lard and lard derivatives are found in some make up products such as eye liners, eyebrow pencils and lipsticks. Lard may also be used in the manufacture of soaps.

RANK #9 – GHEE BUTTER

Nutritional Criteria	Rating
High in Complex Carbohydrates	0
High in Dietary Fibre	0
Low in Saturated Fats	0
High in Monounsaturated Fats	☆☆☆
High in Polyunsaturated Fats	☆☆
Low in Cholesterol	☆☆☆
High in Iron	0
Low in Sodium	☆☆☆☆☆☆☆
High in Potassium	0
High in Calcium	0
High in Vitamin A	☆☆☆☆☆☆
High in Vitamin C	0
High in Vitamin B$_6$	0
High in Folate	0
Zoochemicals	0

GHEE BUTTER

Other Common Name(s): Clarified Butter

Origin and Background

Ghee is a type of butter which has been clarified. The butter is simmered, the top layer of impurities removed, and the clarified layer retained. Spices may be added. Ghee originated in India and is commonly used in Middle Eastern, Indian, and Southeast Asian cuisine. The taste and texture of ghee is determined by the quality of the butter, the milk source used in the process and the duration of time spent boiling.

Ghee should be stored in an airtight container to prevent moisture from deteriorating the product. It should also be kept away from light, such as, sunlight, UV and fluorescent, which can speed up oxidation. It can remain unrefrigerated for up to 3 months. After that time, it should be refrigerated where it can remain for up to a year. It will harden but can be softened once left at room temperature for a while.

Varieties

Ghee can be made from any butter.

Health and Dietary Benefits

Over 60% of the fat in ghee is saturated but its use compared with butter is controversial. Ghee is a good source of vitamin A which is important to the maintenance of the immune system, and for good vision.

Butyrate, a fatty acid, is an important component of ghee and is reported to be associated with an immune system response that soothes inflammation. It has anti-viral properties and helps heal and repair the stomach lining. Individuals with intestinal disorders like Crohn's disease can find this useful.

Preparation and Culinary Uses

Ghee is used in Indian cuisine in rice, curries, on breads such as roti and naan. It is also used in the preparation of sweets. Ghee is well suited for deep fat frying since its smoke point is higher than most vegetable oils. It is also used for sautéing.

Other Uses

Ayurvedic medicine has used ghee regularly to treat burns and swelling. As a topical moisturizer it is used to relieve dry complexions. It can also be applied on the scalp to fight dryness and encourage the growth of thick, lustrous hair. Hindu religious rituals e.g. marriages and funerals usually use ghee.

RANK #10 – BUTTER

Nutritional Criteria	Rating
High in Complex Carbohydrates	0
High in Dietary Fibre	0
Low in Saturated Fats	0
High in Monounsaturated Fats	✩✩
High in Polyunsaturated Fats	✩
Low in Cholesterol	✩✩✩
High in Iron	0
Low in Sodium	✩✩✩✩✩✩✩
High in Potassium	0
High in Calcium	0
High in Vitamin A	✩✩✩✩✩✩
High in Vitamin C	0
High in Vitamin B$_6$	✩
High in Folate	0
Zoochemicals	0

BUTTER

Origin and Background

Butter is an ancient, prepared food, having been made by people at least 4,000 years ago. It is made by churning the cream of milk. Butter will retain its quality better once stored away from heat, air and light. It is therefore recommended to store it well wrapped in the refrigerator. A small amount can be kept outside the refrigerator for use, but it should be well covered. Butter is available either as sticks, blocks or in a container.

Varieties

Butter can be made from the milk of cows, buffalo, goats or sheep. Butter is available in its regular consistency or as whipped butter, made by whipping added milk and regular butter. This product is lighter and easier to spread.

Health and Dietary Benefits

Butter is a high-calorie food due to its fat content. One tablespoon provides about 100 calories. Saturated fats predominate. Mono and poly-unsaturated fatty acids are present in low amounts. Butter also naturally contains a small amount of trans fats. Due to its high calorie content, it is used to increase the caloric content for certain dietary regimens. Butter is also a good source of Vitamin A. Its sodium content varies depending on the brand. In some countries, both regular and unsalted/sweet butter is available, the latter being a better option for persons who must control their dietary sodium intake.

Butter was once considered to be an unhealthy fat but can be included in to the diet when used in moderation.

Preparation and Culinary Uses

Butter is widely used in baking and cooking. It is also used as a spread and to add flavour to soups, sauces, gravies and other dishes.

Fats & Oils

Nutritional Criteria	Avocado (1)	Ackee (2)	Canola Oil (3)	Olive Oil (4)	Soft Margarine (5)	Coconut oil (6)	Vegetable Shortening (7)	Lard (8)	Ghee Butter (9)	Butter (10)
						Summary of Ratings				
High in Complex Carbohydrates	0	0	0	0	0	0	0	0	0	0
High in Dietary Fibre	6	4	0	0	0	0	0	0	0	0
Low in Saturated Fats	6	6	8	7	6	0	0	2	0	0
High in Monounsaturated Fats	7	6	9	9	6	5	4	6	3	2
High in Polyunsaturated Fats	6	2	6	6	6	3	2	4	2	1
Low in Cholesterol	10	10	10	10	10	10	10	4	3	3
High in Iron	0	1	0	0	0	0	0	0	0	0
Low in Sodium	10	8	10	10	7	10	10	10	7	7
High in Potassium	4	4	0	0	0	0	0	0	0	0
High in Calcium	1	4	0	0	0	1	0	0	0	0
High in Vitamin A	2	1	0	0	4	0	0	0	6	6
High in Vitamin C	4	4	0	0	0	0	0	0	0	0
High in Vitamin B$_6$	4	1	0	0	0	0	0	0	0	1
High in Folate	4	1	0	0	0	0	0	0	0	0
Phytochemicals	4	2	3	2	0	2	0	0	0	0

BIBLIOGRAPHY

Ayala Silva T., Ledesma N. (2014) Avocado History, Biodiversity and Production. In: Nandwani D. (eds) Sustainable Horticultural Systems. *Sustainable Development and Biodiversity*, vol 2. Springer, Cham.

Canola Council of Canada https://www.canolacouncil.org/oil-and-meal/what-is-canola/

Cole, J.W. (2019) Processing and Storage Problems of Lard, https://meatscience.org/docs/default-source/publications-resources/rmc/1949/processing-and-storage-problems-of-lard.pdf?sfvrsn=2, Accessed 08 May.

Cosmeticsinfo.org (2016). Lard. The Science & Safety Behind Your Favorite Products. Retrieved From https://www.cosmeticsinfo.org/ingredient/lard

Duarte, P., Chaves, M., Borges, C & Mendonça, C. (2016). Avocado: Characteristics, health benefits and uses. Ciência Rural. 46. 747–754. 10.1590/0103-8478cr20141516.

Dumancas, G, Viswanath, L., Leon, A., Ramasahayam, S., Maples, R., Hikkaduwa, K., Rangika & Don, U., Perera, U. D. Nuwan., Langford, J., Shakir, A & Castles, S. (2016). Health benefits of virgin coconut oil.

Easy Homemade Whipped Butter Recipe | Little Dairy On the ... https://www.little-dairyontheprairie.com/whipped-butter, accessed April 19, 2020

Eyres L., Eyres M.F, Chisholm A., &Brown R.C. (2016). Nutrition Reviews, Coconut oil consumption and cardiovascular risk factors in humans., 74(4):267–80. doi: 10.1093/nutrit/nuw002. Epub 2016 Mar 5.

Goldson, A., Bremmer D., Nelson K. & Minott D.A. (2014). Fat profile of Jamaican ackees, oleic acid content and possible health implications. *West Indian Medical Journal*. 2014; 63:9–12. [PMC free article] [PubMed]

Ganesan, P., Hae-Soo, K. & Al, G. (2013). Butter, Ghee, and Cream Products. 10.1002/9781118534168.ch18.

Henry, F J. "Revisiting plant fats and health in the Caribbean." *The West Indian medical journal* Vol. 63,1 (2014): 1–2. doi:10.7727/wimj.2014.091

Hunter, J.E., Zhang J, Kris-Etherton (201). PM. Cardiovascular disease risk of dietary stearic acid compared with trans, other saturated and unsaturated fatty acids: a systematic review. *Am J Clin Nutr*. 2010;91:46–63. [PubMed]

Kucińska, K. (2018). How to Store Butter and Margarine. Retrieved from https://listonic.com/how-to-store-butter-and-margarine/

Kumar, A. & Naik, S. (2018). Ghee: Its Properties, Importance and Health Benefits.

Marcus, J.B. (2013). Culinary Nutrition, *The Science and Practice of Healthy Cooking*, Pages 231–277 Academic Press.

Rahmani, G., Martin-Smith, J. & Sullivan P. (2017). The Avacado Hand, *Irish Medical Journal*. 18;110(10):658.

Sales-Campos, H. Souza, P.R, Peghini B.C., da Silva, J.S. & Cardoso C.R. (2013). An overview of the modulatory effects of oleic acid in health and disease. *Mimi Rev Med Chem.* 2013; 13:201–210. [PubMed]

Sankararaman, S. & Sferra, T.J. (2018). Are We Going Nuts on Coconut Oil?, Current Nutrition Reports, 2018 Sep;7(3):107–115. doi: 10.1007/s13668-018-0230-5.

Solomon, F.J. (2016). Avocado Production. Government of Trinidad and Tobago, Ministry of Agriculture, Land and Fisheries Extension Training and Information Services Division, Technical Bulletin, TT: AgExt./TB:16:01

United States Department of Agriculture Agricultural Research Service, National Nutrient Database for Standard Reference Legacy Release.

United States Department of Agriculture (USDA) United States Standards for Grades of Olive Oil and Olive-Pomace Oil Effective October 25, 2010, FEDERAL REGISTER April 28, 2010 https://www.ams.usda.gov/sites/default /files/media/Olive_Oil_and _Olive-Pomace_Oil_Standard%5B1%5D.pdf

USDA National Nutrient Database. Retrieved from https://ndb.nal.usda.gov/ ndb/foods/show/12115?fgcd=&manu=&format=&count=&max=25&off-set=&sort=default&order=asc&qlookup=coconut+cream&ds=SR&qt=&qp=&qa-=&qn=&q=&ing=, accessed 09 May 2019

Wallace, T.C. (2019. Health Effects of Coconut Oil-A Narrative Review of Current Evidence., *Journal of the American college of nutrition.* 38(2):97–107. doi: 10.1080/07315724.2018.1497562. Epub 2018 Nov 5

Wang et al. (2016). Association of Specific Dietary Fats with Total and Cause-Specific Mortality, *JAMA Intern Med.* 176(8):1134-1145. doi:10.1001/jamainternmed.2016.2417

Win, T. D. Oleic acid – the anti-breast cancer component in olive oil. AU J T. 2005; 9:75–78.

Zock P.L, (1998). Katan MB. Linoleic acid intake and cancer risk: a review and meta-analysis. *Am J Clin Nutr.* 1998; 68:142–153. [PubMed]

CPSIA information can be obtained
at www.ICGtesting.com
Printed in the USA
BVHW020352250821
615141BV00002B/7